# SLUMS AND SUBURBS

# BOOKS IN THE FIELD OF EDUCATION IN A STUDY OF THE AMERICAN HIGH SCHOOL

by James Bryant Conant

*The American High School Today*
*The Child, the Parent, and the State*
*Education in the Junior High School Years*
*Slums and Suburbs*

# SLUMS AND SUBURBS

### A Commentary on Schools in Metropolitan Areas

## JAMES BRYANT CONANT

*McGRAW-HILL BOOK COMPANY, INC.*
*New York    Toronto    London*

# SLUMS AND SUBURBS

Library of Congress Catalog Card Number: 61–16929

Sixth Printing

# ACKNOWLEDGMENT

The present volume is based primarily on observations made during my study of education in the junior high school years, which was financed by a grant from the Carnegie Corporation of New York to the Educational Testing Service of Princeton, New Jersey. The results of that inquiry have been published elsewhere. Those who assisted me were Messrs. M. P. Gaffney, F. O. White, and E. A. Dunham. I am indebted to them for their contributions to this book, particularly to Mr. Dunham, who rewrote and rearranged a considerable portion of the first draft and collaborated closely with me in the preparation of the final manuscript.

*James B. Conant*

*A Study of the American High School*
  *588 Fifth Avenue*
  *New York 36, N.Y.*

*June 14, 1961*

# CONTENTS

# SLUMS AND SUBURBS

# INTRODUCTION

This is a book of contrasts. I shall present a picture of two totally different kinds of neighborhoods and the public schools which serve them. I shall discuss city slums and wealthy suburbs. In the large metropolitan areas of New York, Philadelphia, Detroit, Chicago, and St. Louis, one has no difficulty in locating examples of both. In some cases twenty minutes' or half an hour's drive will enable a person to go from one to the other. A visit to the high school serving each community will open the eyes of a visitor to the complexities of American public education. Within the limitation imposed by the budget, the schools in the two totally different neighborhoods may be doing a good job. Yet their basic problems are in many respects quite unlike. And the differences spring from the differences in the nature of the families being served. One lesson to be drawn from visiting and contrasting a well-to-do suburb and a slum is all important for understanding American public education. *The lesson is that to a considerable degree what a school should do and can do is determined by the status and ambitions of the families being served.*

In the suburban high school from which 80 per cent or more of the graduates enter some sort of college, the most important problem from the parents' point of view is to ensure the admission of their children to prestige colleges; consequently there is great concern over good teaching of academic subjects. From the educator's point of view, however, the most vexing problem is to adjust the family's ambitions to the boy's or girl's abilities. In the city slum, where as many as a half of the children drop out of school in grades 9, 10, and 11, the problems are almost the reverse of those facing the principal and guidance officer of the rich suburban school. The task with which the school people in the slum must struggle is, on the one hand, to prepare a student for getting and keeping a job as soon as he leaves school and, on the other hand, to encourage those who have academic talent to aim at a profession through higher education. The task thus stated seems simple. In actual fact the difficulties are appalling. So appalling, indeed, that as I prepared to spell them out in my final report to the Carnegie Corporation, I decided to write a small book devoted largely to their consideration.

I have done so because I am convinced we are allowing social dynamite to accumulate in our large cities. I am not nearly so concerned about the plight of suburban parents whose offspring are having difficulty finding places in prestige colleges as I am about the plight of parents in the slums whose children either drop out or graduate from school without prospects of either further education or employment. In some slum neighborhoods I have no doubt that over a half of the boys between sixteen and twenty-one are out of school and out of work. Leaving aside human tragedies, I submit that a continuation of this situation is a menace to the social and political health of the large cities.

The improvement of slum conditions is only in part a question of improving education. But the role of the schools is of the utmost importance. As I hope to make clear in later pages, the school authorities ought to be given the responsibility for helping out-of-school youth between the ages of sixteen and twenty-one both to further their education and gain employment. Added responsibilities, however, require additional funds. Indeed the whole problem of financing public education in the large cities is a major national concern.

The contrast in money available to the schools in a

wealthy suburb and to the schools in a large city jolts one's notions of the meaning of equality of opportunity. The pedagogic tasks which confront the teachers in the slum schools are far more difficult than those which their colleagues in the wealthy suburbs face. Yet the expenditure per pupil in the wealthy suburban school is as high as $1,000 per year. The expenditure in a big city school is less than half that amount. An even more significant contrast is provided by looking at the school facilities and noting the size of the professional staff. In the suburb there is likely to be a spacious modern school staffed by as many as 70 professionals per 1,000 pupils; in the slum one finds a crowded, often dilapidated and unattractive school staffed by 40 or fewer professionals per 1,000 pupils. The contrast challenges any complacency we may have about our method of financing public schools—even within a rich state like New York.

In the first three chapters of this volume I present a picture of the schools in the slums of the big cities that my staff and I have visited. Then follows a discussion of the very different problems facing the school authorities in some of the well-to-do suburbs in large metropolitan complexes. These areas include the ten largest cities in the nation—New York, Chicago, Los Angeles, Philadelphia, Detroit, Baltimore, Houston, Cleveland, Washington, and St. Louis. Within each area, one finds, of course, a broad spectrum of communities, and I am presenting the picture only of the extremes. In doing so I shall confine myself to public school problems, leaving aside the important fact that parochial schools in the large cities enroll a large fraction of the school population—a third or more in many cities.

My first report dealt with the comprehensive high school in small independent cities that were not part of a metropolitan complex. I classify as independent such cities as Elkhart, Indiana, Mansfield, Ohio, and Bakersfield, California, because in terms of their economic and social life they are largely self-sufficient. With a population of 10,000 to 60,000, such a city generally has only one senior high school. It may or may not have a local community college. Because the city is an industrial center, the shop facilities in the high school will be used at night for an extensive apprentice program for high school graduates. Employment opportunities are, for the most part, local. A labor-management committee advises in regard to the various programs offered with federal Smith–Hughes funds, including the programs in grades 11 and 12 in the high school. The school board represents the entire community, and under favorable conditions the parents and various civic groups feel that the schools are honestly run for the benefit of all. Indeed the citizens may feel great pride in their school, although, alas, this pride is all too often symbolized by the marching bands and the successful football and basketball teams.

In the small independent cities and the consolidated rural districts the widely comprehensive high school functions as an effective instrument of democracy. All the youth in the community are enrolled and there is a variety of elective programs. These are reasons why I chose to focus my attention on such schools in preparing my first report. Any school that enrolls most of the youth in the community can be said to be comprehensive. The degree of comprehensiveness turns on the variety of elective programs. The metropolitan areas of the country, the subject of the present volume, are almost without high schools that, in regard to the curriculum, are widely comprehensive. This is true whether one turns to a suburb or, with few exceptions, to a large central city. What do I mean by this statement? I mean that it is difficult for a youth in a metropolitan area to find high schools which offer a wide range of significant vocational programs—unless he goes to specialized technical or vocational high schools. In the suburbs there is relatively little demand for vocational education. In the big city there are no labor-management advisory committees comparable to those characteristic of the small independent cities. Those that exist serve the vocational high schools; the employment area is too large, diverse, and complicated to be surveyed by any one committee.

In no school district within a great metropolitan area is there the sense of social and economic cohesion such as one finds in a small city. One has only to note the difference in the composition of the Rotary Club to see what I have in mind. The leading Rotarians in the small independent city usually live and have their principal business in the city. The community, while socially heterogeneous, is yet a viable social and economic unit. In a suburban town or city, however, the Rotary Club is often composed of those who are not the richest or the most influential business and professional men in the community, because the business leaders who live in the suburbs work in the city and may belong to the Rotary Club in the city.

Perhaps some may think these differences trivial. I assure the reader that in terms of understanding public education they are not. They are significant both on their own account and as evidence as to the kinds of school districts which the public secondary schools must serve in the metropolitan areas. They affect the financing of the school, the composition of the school board, the relation of the parents to the school, and the chief problems of the elementary as well as the secondary school.

I estimate that a third of the high school population of the country resides in the large metropolitan areas, but by no means all this number attend the prosperous suburban schools. Nor do all in the large cities within these areas attend slum schools. Many high schools within each city are, except for the vocational programs, very much like the comprehensive schools which are described in *The American High School Today* and which enroll a third of the high school population. Finally, a third of the high school population still attends high schools, generally in rural areas, that are too small to offer satisfactory education, particularly to the more able students. Though enrolling only a third of the student population, these schools represent 80 per cent of all public high schools in the United States. The number one problem in many states is elimination of small schools by further district consolidation. I should not like to attempt to match the seriousness of this problem on a national basis with the problem of the big city slum schools on which I am focusing attention in this book. They both present challenges to our American belief in the principle of equality of educational opportunity. Only through aroused public sentiment can these and related pressing problems be solved to the benefit of the public welfare of the United States.

# CHAPTER I

## City Slums and Negro Education

In this and the next two chapters I shall consider the special educational problems facing school boards, administrators, and teachers in the big central cities of our largest metropolitan areas—especially New York, Chicago, Detroit, Philadelphia, and St. Louis.

In each one of these cities one can find neighborhoods composed of various minority groups. Many of these are areas now designated as "culturally deprived" or "culturally different," but in my youth they would have been more simply designated as "slums." In particular one finds large Negro neighborhoods and often somewhat smaller areas made up entirely of Negro slums. The schools serving such neighborhoods must be visited in order for one to understand the nature of the difficult tasks which the teachers face.

### The Status of the Negro

The slum areas of certain big Northern cities are today largely inhabited by Negroes who have recently moved from the South hoping to improve their lot. The economic changes in the South which have forced this migration are too well known to require elaboration. The Negro is being displaced as a farm laborer and, being unable because of discrimination to obtain other employment in the section where he was born, he becomes a migrant headed North. Between 1950 and 1960 the percentage of Negroes living in the South dropped from 60 to 52 per cent. St. Louis is said to be the first stopping point for many who make the journey, though the school people in Chicago, Detroit, Philadelphia, Washington, and New York indicate that their problems with the recently arrived Negroes from the South are quite as great as those which confront their colleagues in St. Louis. New York State now has the largest Negro population of any state in the Union.

Since I am going to be completely frank about Negro education in the largest cities, it may be well to take a few paragraphs to set forth my own interpretation of the distressing history of the Negro in the United States. At the outset I must make it plain that I approach the delicate and complex problem of interrace relations with the background of a one hundred per cent New Englander. My family tradition was that of the strong abolitionists. My mother, who remembered the Civil War, used to say that as a child she was brought up to think Negroes were if anything better than white people. It is as difficult for me to imagine myself in the position of the well-educated Southerner who in the 1850s argued for Negro slavery as it is for me to understand how intelligent Germans in the 1930s ardently supported Hitler. Yet the fact of the matter is that in the eighteenth and first half of the nineteenth centuries a great many citizens of the United States with high principles and broad education believed that "the peculiar institution of the South" was not only constitutionally justified but morally correct.

As I read the history of the United States, this republic was born with a congenital defect—Negro slavery. Or, if one prefers another metaphor, we started life under a curse from which we are not yet free. To be sure, slavery was recognized by at least some of the Founding Fathers as an abominable inheritance from the past. Many hoped the institution would disappear within a generation. We must remember, however, that even the author of the Declara-

tion of Independence, who advocated emancipation, a[...]
advocated the colonization of the freed Negro slave *outside* the United States. For otherwise, he said, "Deep-rooted
prejudices entertained by the whites; ten thousand recollec-
tions by the blacks of the injuries they have sustained; new
provocations; the real distinctions which nature has made;
and many other circumstances, will divide us into parties,
and produce convulsions, which will probably never end
but in the extermination of the one or the other race." The
idea of the Negro and the white living together peacefully
on equal terms in a free society was literally inconceivable
to Jefferson. Yet after nearly two hundred years we are
endeavoring to accomplish the building of just that type
of society. We make a great mistake, I believe, if we fail to
recognize the rough and weary road we have had to travel
in our attempt as a free and independent people to remove
the social consequence of the inherited curse of Negro
slavery.

In spite of the acceptance of the principles of the Dec-
laration of Independence, the makers of the Constitution
wrote in the fugitive-slave provision as part of the compromise to satisfy the South, and as late as 1813 Congress
explicitly referred to "citizens of the United States *or* persons of color, native of the United States," thus emphasiz-
ing that freed Negro slaves were not citizens. The Mis-
souri Compromise, "bleeding" Kansas, the Dred Scott decision of the Supreme Court in 1857, the devastation of the
Civil War, Lincoln's Emancipation Proclamation, the Thir-
teenth and Fourteenth Amendments—these are but a few
of the historic markers of the truly frightful journey of a
people believing in the novel doctrine of the American
Revolution yet caught in the morass of Negro slavery.
After the victory of the North, a vindictive Congressional
majority tried first to solve with force a moral and socio-
logical problem and then gave up. The people of the United
States through their duly elected representatives in Con-

:d for generations in the establishment of a
em as a substitute for Negro slavery. A ma-
Supreme Court struck down what attempts
use the federal power to loosen the bonds of
and supported a doctrine of equal but sep-
As recently as 1932 a national commission
d a leading Negro educator spoke of im-
proving the education of the Negro entirely in terms of obtaining federal support for separate schools. Equal educational facilities were demanded but not a word was written about desegregation.

As one reviews the events of the last hundred years
and squarely faces a multitude of unpleasant facts today,
the temptation to indulge in the fantasy of rewriting history arises. I cannot help regretting that the "black Repub-
licans" of the 1860s, by being so revengeful, precipitate,
and corrupt in their attempts at reconstruction, prevented
the moderate group from constructive acts favorable to
the status of the Negro. If Congress had acted favorably
on President Grant's recommendations of 1875 and the
necessary number of states had agreed, an amendment to
the Constitution would then and there have established
a federal policy as to public education. Each state would
have been required to maintain free public schools open
to all irrespective of race, color, or creed, and, interest-
ingly, no public funds at any level could have been used
for the "benefit or aid, directly, or indirectly, of any re-
ligious sect or denomination. . . ." Even if the presence
of federal troops had been necessary to get such a system
of desegregated schools under way, the ultimate result
would, to my mind, have justified this harsh reconstruction measure—"making it the duty of each of the several
States to establish and forever maintain free public schools
adequate to the education of all the children in the rudi-
mentary branches within their respective limits." Today
any state, by changing its constitution, could close all its

public schools—both segregated and integrated schools—and there is little that could be done at the federal level to prevent it.

As we now recognize so plainly, but so belatedly, a caste system finds its clearest manifestation in an educational system. By the same token, in the critical days when slavery had just vanished and caste lines were not yet established on a new basis, a system of free public schools for Negroes and whites together might have softened the caste lines even if a majority of pupils attended all-white or all-Negro schools. Above all, the existence of such schools, guaranteed by the power of the federal government, might have assured the eventual establishment of a corps of Negro and white teachers working together for the betterment of the recently liberated Negro slaves. To be sure, most of the white teachers would have come from the Northern states at first, and normal schools for both races would have been required. The principle of an integrated teaching staff, however, would have been established. And once such a staff had been established in at least some of the former Confederate states, the whole problem of Negro education would have been viewed in a different light.

I might note parenthetically that the significance of the status of the Negro teacher is not always fully appreciated by those who discuss the Negro problem. Yet what differentiates Chicago from Atlanta, let us say, is not only that there are mixed schools as well as all-Negro schools in the Northern city, but that one finds a dedicated group of Negro and white teachers working together harmoniously on a set of difficult tasks. In a Southern city, the most one finds are formal conferences of the Negro and white teaching staffs; and often such conferences, quite common before the Supreme Court decision in 1954, are no longer held because of the state of public opinion.

The "might have beens" of the past are probably profitless to consider. Segregated schools and staffs were

established all through the South. The Constitution of
the United States was not amended. For nearly a hundred
years our ancestors—North and South, East and West—
accepted, almost without protest, the transformation of
the status of the Negro from that of a slave into that of a
member of a lower, quite separate caste. The present situation is a consequence of a national policy, or rather the lack
of a national education policy, which has persisted for
generations. We now struggle with the consequences, and
one of these is the situation in the Northern cities to which
I am directing the attention of the reader.

I shall not discuss education in those many communities where segregation is still the policy of the school
authorities. In all the cities to which I shall refer, the schools
either have been desegregated for generations or were
desegregated shortly after the decisions of the Supreme
Court in 1954 and 1955.

## Aptitude and Background

Before proceeding with this discussion, I must insert a few
paragraphs to dispose of a common fallacy which one often
hears privately even in the North. This is to the effect that
it has been clearly established that a colored student on the
average is inherently inferior to a white student. No such
generalization has been established, and in my view the
difficulties in obtaining evidence that would validate or,
for that matter, clearly negate such a position are virtually
insurmountable. However, it has been established beyond
any reasonable doubt that community and family background play a large role in determining scholastic aptitude
and school achievement. Anyone who thinks they do not
simply has not visited widely among American schools.

Within such a city as Chicago, or Detroit, or New
York, for example, the figures showing the distribution
of scores on scholastic aptitude tests in different neigh-

borhoods are most revealing. In one of these cities the average score of the eighth-grade pupils in a school in a relatively well-to-do, stable residential section is 123; in another neighborhood of about the same size but composed entirely of people of low socio-economic status, the average score is only 76. The average score city-wide is 100. It is true that in the section that shows up so poorly in these scholastic aptitude tests there are many, many Negroes. But there is no way of deciding whether the low score is related to the color of the pupils' skins or the low socio-economic condition of the entire group.

A very important fact not to be overlooked is that the comparison of average scores leaves out of account the overlap of scores that, as far as I know, is found whenever such comparisons are made. There are always some Negroes who score better than most whites and some whites who score lower than most Negroes. Important, too, is the fact that such a test correlates highly with reading ability. Children who for one reason or another have learned to read will do better on this kind of test than children who have not learned. In the suburban school practically all the children read well; in the slum school few do.

In view of the influence of cultural background, a word is in order on the validity of the commonly used "intelligence" or scholastic aptitude tests. In recent years, the paper-and-pencil tests measuring intelligence or scholastic aptitude have often been attacked because they are considered to be unfair to underprivileged children. Indeed the whole concept of intelligence tests is distasteful to some Negro educators whom I have met, not only because the test which is commonly used to measure I.Q.s reflects the cultural level of the family, but also because the whole idea of an intelligence quotient is considered too deterministic. To assign an I.Q. to a child at an early age is to brand the child. On the last point, I think one must admit that, as originally developed and used by many educators in the 1920s and 1930s, intelligence tests were thought of as measuring the inherent or genetic qualities of the individual. The evidence at first available seemed to indicate that the chances of a single individual's I.Q. changing over the years were slight. Today, however, when we tend to think of paper-and-pencil intelligence tests, at least in the higher grades, as measuring a type of scholastic aptitude, we are well aware that we are measuring an aptitude which in part has been developed in the school. The difference between an I.Q. test and a good achievement test is one of degree not kind. Understood in this sense and with evidence accumulating that an individual's aptitude score may change during his school years, there is nothing deterministic about the use of the various forms of intelligence or aptitude tests which are on the market. If they are understood only as giving a prediction of *probability* of academic success in subsequent schoolwork, they are no more and no less influenced by home or other environmental factors than are the marks for schoolwork given by a conscientious teacher.

In this regard, one wonders at the purpose that would be served by establishing so-called culture-free tests which, it is asserted, would discount the cultural bias in the group paper-and-pencil intelligence tests. Whether such a test can be devised is itself a question. Granting that one could have a test that showed equal results with children of widely divergent socio-economic backgrounds, the results would serve little useful purpose, since schools exist in a society that does have cultural biases. As a knowledgeable person in testing has said, "If a child does poorly on an aptitude test because he comes from the wrong side of the tracks, it isn't the test that is being 'unfair,' it is the hard facts of social circumstance that are unfair. Anyone who is seriously interested in improving the lot of the culturally underprivileged should direct his attention not to changing the tests—which would accomplish literally nothing—but to improving the quality of educational opportunity for all children."

Whenever aptitude test scores are cited, it must be borne in mind that their *only* valid use is to make rough predictions of future success in academic work in school. On this basis, most of the pupils in the Negro slum school will have a very difficult time with their future schooling. This is not to say that no effort should be made to upgrade both the aspirations and achievements of slum children. Quite the contrary; good teachers are never defeatists. Dedicated school people in city slums in every city have the goal in mind to raise the sights, ambitions, and academic skills of children with low scores on tests of scholastic aptitude. They have this goal precisely because they realize that even though the betting odds are against their success, there is always a chance that at least some boys and girls with hopeless school backgrounds and low I.Q. scores will show dramatic progress. This happens time and again—but more of these success stories in later chapters. At this point, let me say that although it is my belief that students should take as wide a program of academic studies as they can handle, one must not be deluded into thinking that miracles can be worked with any large numbers of children. Aptitude test scores, marks of conscientious teachers, achievement test results—these reliable predictors of academic success indicate the enormity of the task of teachers in slum schools.

In considering the relative abilities of whites and Negroes, let us examine the situation in an *all-white* slum in a city of considerable size. Perhaps the greatest handicap to good school work is the high mobility of the population in the neighborhood. It is not uncommon in such a school to have a turnover of the entire enrollment in one school year. A careful study of a group of children in grade 4 of one such school showed that their average achievement level was a full year below their grade placement—a typical situation in any slum area.

What the teachers in this school have to contend with is shown by a report from the principal, who writes:

"When a residential area composed of large, old homes formerly occupied by owners and single family groups changes economically and socially, conditions of general deterioration begin. Absentee owners rent the property by single rooms or small so-called apartments of two or three rooms to large families. . . . Such conditions attract transients (who either cannot or will not qualify for supervised low income housing), the unemployed, the unskilled and unschooled, and the distressed families whose breadwinners have either just been committed to prisons or mental institutions or who have but recently been released from such. The only possession most of these families have is children. . . . In such an environment all forms of evil flourish—the peddling of dope, drunkenness, disease, accidents, truancies, physical, mental and moral handicaps, sex perversions involving children. . . .

"The parents of at least one-third of the children are either in penal institutions, are on probation, or have prison records. At least 100 children are on probation to the Juvenile Court. There has not been a day since I've been at the school that there has not been one or more children in detention at the Juvenile Court. . . .

"Unless a school is able to educate its children so they may become competent and responsible citizens its work is a temporary stopgap that relieves immediate suffering only. Although the school is the only organization that has instruction as its primary responsibility, when a noble hearted teacher faces a barefoot, hungry, sick, distressed child, the result is an endless chain of efforts to relieve such a child.

"We realize that little or nothing can be done for or with the parents of the children who face such serious problems in their homes. These problems directly affect the child's health, attendance, emotional and personal adjustment, his learning and his progress (or lack of it) in every respect. In all probability at least one-half of our children will be school dropouts. In our opinion the children need, desperately, for desirable development, in addition to good schools—good homes, churches and communities."

I am quoting from an official report which, in acknowledging the generally low achievement of the white children in this school, makes the interesting statement that "There is no reason to believe that these students as a group are inherently or genetically less capable than average students, but apparently because of some types of experiences in their lives they have been unable to develop their intellectual skills." The belief expressed in the first part of this sentence can hardly be based on anything firmer than an assumption as to the genetic uniformity of white children whose ancestors have for several generations lived in the United States. Such an assumption, of course, leaves out of account the possibility of a selective process occurring over the generations as some tended to move to one type of occupation and settle in one type of community. However, since I see no way of investigating the role of selective migration, I would be inclined to let the assumption stand unchallenged. *Only I would argue strongly that to date we have no evidence to indicate that the assumption should not be broadened to include* both *white and Negro students.* For all the contrary evidence, namely the poor work in school and low scores on tests made by Negroes, is based to a large degree on the performance of children in what are essentially slum conditions.

In short, until we have a great deal more data about test scores and school records, especially with respect to large numbers of Negro children from stable high-income communities, I for one would reserve judgment as to the answer to the question whether there is a correlation between race and scholastic aptitude. And until the evidence is available, I suggest the only assumption to use as a working hypothesis is that there is *no* genetic or inherent difference as far as aptitude for schoolwork is concerned between large numbers of Negroes in the United States and large numbers of other children.

## Elementary Schools in Negro Slums

With this background sketched in, I can now take up the educational problems in the Negro slums of certain of our largest cities. I wish that I could do more than take them up. What I should like to do is to create in the reader's mind a feeling of anxiety and concern. For without being an alarmist, I must say that when one considers the total situation that has been developing in the Negro city slums since World War II, one has reason to worry about the future. The building up of a mass of unemployed and frustrated Negro youth in congested areas of a city is a social phenomenon that may be compared to the piling up of inflammable material in an empty building in a city block. Potentialities for trouble—indeed possibilities of disaster—are surely there.

Let me describe a slum that might be in any one of several of the large cities I have visited. The inhabitants are all Negroes and with few exceptions have entered the city from a state in the deep South anytime within the last month to the last three years. Often the composition of a school grade in such an area will alter so rapidly that a teacher will find at the end of a school year that she is teaching but few pupils who started with her in the fall. I recall the principal of one school stating that a teacher absent more than one week will have difficulty recognizing her class when she returns. This comes about because mothers move with their offspring from one rented room to another from month to month and in so doing often go from one elementary school district to another; I am told that resident tenements look more like transient hotels. I write "mothers" advisedly, since in one neighborhood, by no means the worst I have seen, a questionnaire sent out by the school authorities indicated that about a third of the pupils came from family units (one hesitates to use the word "home") which had no father, stepfather, or male guardian. This particular section was by no means homogeneous, of course. For while many moved about from room to room, a quarter of the parents reported that they owned their homes. Only 10 per cent of the parents had graduated from high school and only 33 per cent had completed the elementary school. Contrast the situation in which a third of the parents have completed elementary school with that in a high-income suburb where as many as 90 per cent of the parents have bachelor's degrees, if not graduate degrees from a university.

These Negro slums seem to vary considerably with respect to the social mores. In some there are very bad gangs with gang warfare among the boys. There are also vicious fights outside of school between Negro girls. The condition in one such neighborhood was summed up to one of my staff by a principal of a junior high school who said even he was shocked by the answers to a questionnaire to the girls which asked what was their biggest problem. The majority replied to the effect that their biggest problem was getting from the street into their apartment without being molested in the hallway of the tenement. He went on to say that the area had a set of social customs of its own. The women, on the whole, work and earn fairly good wages, but the male Negro often earns less than the woman and would rather not work at all than to be in this situation. As a consequence, the streets are full of unemployed men who hang around and prey on the girls. The women are the centers of the family and as a rule are extremely loyal to the children. The men, on the other hand, are floaters, and many children have no idea who their father is. Similar reports from principals and teachers can be heard by the attentive and sympathetic visitor to the Negro slums of

any one of several cities. Racial discrimination on the part
of employers and labor unions is certainly one factor which
leads to the existence of so many male Negro floaters.
What is terrifying is that the number of male *youth*
in this category is increasing almost daily.

I have so far referred only to white and Negro slums.
A few words are necessary to point out that in some cities,
New York in particular, there are slum areas inhabited by
recent arrivals from Puerto Rico. In these sections, the
problems are similar to those I have been describing but
complicated by the difference in language. Unlike the
American Negro from the South, these recent arrivals
bring with them a set of social mores closely associated with
their own methods of communication. At the same time,
they often, if not always, come with children whose schooling has been bad. Clearly the task of educating these Puerto
Rican children involves both a reading and a foreign language problem. These problems are so special I shall not
attempt to discuss them here. One hardly needs to point out
that their existence adds one more complication to the tasks
confronting the administrators and teachers in the New
York City schools. Add to these problems the possibilities
of interracial hostility and gang warfare between Negroes
and Puerto Ricans and the resentment of both toward the
whites, and one has a veritable witches' brew which comes
to boil with unsavory violence in certain schools in certain
areas—particularly in the junior high school years. The
amazing feature of the whole situation is that pupils make
any progress in schools in some areas of the city.

One needs only to visit such a school to be convinced
that the nature of the community largely determines what
goes on in the school. Therefore to attempt to divorce
the school from the community is to engage in unrealistic
thinking, which might lead to policies that could wreak
havoc with the school and the lives of children. The community and the school are inseparable. For example, I have

walked through school corridors in slum areas and, looking
into classrooms, have seen children asleep with their heads
on their hands. Is this situation the result of poor teachers
without either disciplinary control or teaching ability? No,
the children asleep at their desks have been up all night
with no place to sleep or else have been subject to incredibly
violent family fights and horrrors through the night. Check-
ing into one case, a principal told one of my staff that after
climbing six flights of a tenement he found the boy's home
—one filthy room with a bed, a light bulb, and a sink. In
the room lived the boy's mother and her four children. I
might add that it is not unusual for teachers in these schools
to take home with them children with no place to go at
night. The social attitudes found in this kind of slum neigh-
borhod are bound to affect the atmosphere of the school.
As one Negro teacher said to me, "We do quite well
with these children in the lower grades. Each of us is, for
the few hours of the school day, an acceptable substitute
for the mother. But when they reach about 10, 11, or 12
years of age, we lose them. At that time the 'street' takes
over. In terms of schoolwork, progress ceases; indeed many
pupils begin to go backward in their studies!"

I ask the readers of this volume, many of whom live
in wealthy suburbs, to ponder the contrast between the
lives and the education of their children and the lives and
education of the boys and girls in the neighborhoods I
have been describing. It is after visits to schools like these
that I grow impatient with both critics and defenders of
public education who ignore the realities of school situations to engage in fruitless debate about educational philosophy, purposes, and the like. These situations call for
action, not hair-splitting arguments.

Those who are deeply concerned with the education
of the children in these slum areas are not waiting for
others to change the social setting in which the schools
operate. They are tackling the problem of getting the boys

and girls from the poorest families to learn to read and write and do arithmetic. Foreign languages in grade 7 or algebra in grade 8 (recommendations in my junior high school report) have little place in a school in which half the pupils in that grade read at the fourth grade level or below. Homework has little relevance in a situation where home is a filthy, noisy tenement. Discipline, of course, is a problem. Many educators would doubtless be shocked by the practice of on-the-spot demotion of one full academic year, with no questions asked, for all participants in fights. In one junior high school I know of, a very able principal found so intolerable a situation that he established that very rule. As a consequence, there are fewer fights in his school among the boys, many of whom at one time or another have been in trouble with the police. In this school and in many others like it one finds the boys wearing ties and jackets to school, if not their one Sunday suit. When spoken to in the classroom, they rise to recite. Passing time between classes may be as short as one minute in order to preserve order in the halls. The school attempts to bring some kind of order to otherwise chaotic lives. And what is important, this formal atmosphere, at least in one school I know of, appears to work. School spirit has developed, and efforts are now being made to enlist the interest of the parents in the education of their children, who must stay in school till they are sixteen and whom the school will try to keep in school till graduation to prevent unemployed, out-of-school youth from roaming the streets.

In contrast to what one hears about "blackboard jungles," I think I am fairly safe in saying that the outward manifestations of discipline, order, and formal dress are found to a greater degree in the well-run slum schools of a city than they are in the wealthier sections of the same city. The contrast is especially noticeable between city slum schools and wealthy suburban schools, where informality in dress, deportment, and classroom procedure is the rule.

I doubt that many suburban parents would stand for the regimentation and formal discipline meted out in many slum schools. It is not accidental that that part of the progressive movement in education which rebelled against formalism and authoritarianism found root in the suburban and private schools.

I should like to record at this point my impression of what my colleagues and I have seen in slum sections of big cities. Almost without exception we have seen white and Negro teachers and administrators struggling tenaciously and bravely against the adverse influences of the home and the street. As one of my associates who had spent the best years of his life as a principal of a suburban public high school put it, "I visited junior high schools in New York City in some of the worst areas. I expected to find blackboard jungles; instead I found schools with high morale, tight discipline, imaginative principals and teachers. My visits to New York City junior high schools," he went on to say, "have provided some of the most interesting and exciting experiences I have had. In bad neighborhoods with children from hopeless backgrounds these schools are really doing a magnificent job." My own visits were largely confined to similar schools in Chicago, Detroit, and St. Louis, and my admiration for what is being done in those cities is equal to that of my colleague for what he saw in New York City.

## The Importance of the Home

In the slum school, the development of reading skill is obviously of first importance. The earlier the slow readers are spotted and remedial measures instituted, the better. Indeed, the same rule applies as well to any school, but in the heavily college-oriented suburb, the number of slow readers is relatively small and teaching children to read by no means looms so large and difficult a problem as it does in the slums. Some commentators have failed to recognize the relation of the reading problem to the socio-economic and cultural level of the home. Evidence on this point is found in the large cities. Essentially the same methods are used in all the elementary schools in a city, and yet the average grade level of reading in the sixth grade, for example, may vary as much as two grades from one school to another. Concern with improving the reading of the pupils, particularly the slow reader, must continue well beyond the elementary school.

Different administrators and teachers in various cities are tackling the problem of teaching reading in somewhat different ways. My associates and I were very favorably impressed by the effort that was being made in many of the cities we visited. Just how far up the reading scale one can hope to bring the majority of pupils in a slum neighborhood is an open question. The factors working against all forms of intellectual effort are powerful negative influences to overcome. Since the degree of influence of these negative factors varies from child to child even in the same neighborhood, and the neighborhood's social climate changes from year to year, sometimes from month to month, it would be very difficult to obtain significant figures if an analysis of the social factors were attempted. One can only report that in spite of the Herculean efforts which are being made, there are many ninth-grade students in certain large city schools—in some as many as a half—who are reading at a sixth-grade level or lower. It must be remembered, however, that because of the high family mobility very few of these youth have had the advantage of the special attention given to reading in the lower grades in the same city.

In one school I visited, the teachers themselves, mostly Negroes, felt that the only way to improve the reading of the children in the first three or four grades was to do something with their mothers. If the head of the family unit could be located and brought into communication with the school, attempts were made to stimulate an interest in newspapers, magazines, and possibly even books. One of the troubles, the teachers said, is that when the children leave the school they never see anyone read anything—not even newspapers. "If we could change the family attitude toward reading, we could accomplish much." With this statement one must heartily agree and likewise agree that even a slight change, which was all that was expected, would probably be reflected in the reading ability of the children.

In other all-Negro schools, this point was made again and again. Therefore many such schools use social workers or visiting teachers to keep the parent or parents in touch with the school. This is not always an easy task, for the almost illiterate parent may be frightened of anyone officially connected with education. But if the parents can be induced to adopt a positive attitude toward the school, a first step has been taken. If the reading of some sort of printed material can be started, the way is open for the more usual forms of adult education courses. It may be that only by a greatly increased expenditure of funds on adult education can the present blocks to children's educational progress be removed in the most depressed areas of the large cities. Trials of new procedures and imaginative approaches to a complex social and educational problem are certainly in order.

In connection with the difficult task of teaching reading, it is well worth pointing out that without the development of modern testing what is now being accomplished would be quite impossible. I am convinced that fifty years ago in all communities, and even fifteen years ago in many schools, the slow reader was not identified or, if identified, was just ignored. Today in all the larger school systems, reading tests are given in most grades, and the reading level of each pupil and the average of each grade are carefully recorded. This procedure has proved its value. Unlike the

I.Q. scores, it is clear what the reading level tests try to measure. Furthermore there is a mass of evidence that, by remedial work, a child may improve his standing on such a test. What is of prime significance in all the larger schools is that remedial measures *are* taken to improve the reading level of those who have some ability but are far behind the average for their age.

At the risk of being unduly repetitious, I must emphasize that for the last few pages I have been discussing, for the most part, Negro *slums*. To suppose that all Negroes live in such neighborhoods, even in the large cities, would be to make a totally unwarranted inference from what I have reported. A trained sociologist would perhaps be able to characterize every block of city tenements in terms of a series of concepts developed in recent years by his colleagues. Presumably to do so would require an extensive survey. As a first approximation to the data which would be thus obtained, one can use the information supplied by the principals of the public schools serving the different, and usually adjacent, Negro neighborhoods. Particularly significant are the reading levels, the scholastic aptitudes and achievements in grades 7 and 8, and the dropout rate after grade 8. Using such criteria, I know that one will find gradations of Negro neighborhoods in a number of the large cities, just as one finds a similar gradation in white neighborhoods—running from slums to well-to-do residential sections. Furthermore, in some sections of some cities, at least the upper grades will be mixed white and Negro, reflecting, of course a mixture of races in the larger geographic area from which the upper grades draw their pupils. In such schools, I am told, it is usual to find far more whites than Negroes in the group that scores high on aptitude and achievement tests. At first sight such facts might be taken as evidence as to the inherent superiority of the white children for academic work, but anyone who has observed even casually the situation of the Negro in the large cities and who knows the influence of the family on the school performance of the children will see the fallacy of any such conclusion. The position of the family in the *total* community, in this case the entire city, and the past performance of the friends and relatives of the family in getting a job and obtaining recognition enormously affect the attitude of the parents toward intellectual tasks and the desires and ambitions of the children.

## De Facto Segregation

In concluding this chapter, I should like to turn to a thorny subject of great concern to those interested in improving Negro education. This is the question of whether or not *de facto* segregation, as some like to call it, is detrimental to the education of the Negro. Closely related is a second question; namely, should the school authorities endeavor to move Negro children into purely white schools in order to have as many mixed schools as possible? The issue is a very real one, and in a sense it is primarily political. At this point I must make reference to the Supreme Court decisions of 1954 and 1955 because of a tendency to regard them not only as the law of the land but as a sacred text on education. Clearly even a unanimous opinion of the Supreme Court fails to determine educational policy except within the framework set by the issues before the Court —in this case, the "segregation of children in public schools solely on the basis of race." It is necessary to point out this obvious fact, for I have heard the statement made that because the Supreme Court expressed the opinion that "Separate educational facilities are inherently unequal," all completely Negro schools are morally wrong and that there is essentially no difference between *de jure* segregation still found in almost all Southern communities and what some call *de facto* segregation in portions of the large

Northern cities. The point is important and deserves discussion.

If one turns to the Supreme Court decision in the case of *Brown et al. v. Board of Education of Topeka* [347 U.S. 483 (1954)], one finds the sentence I have just quoted about separate educational facilities. Taken out of context, the conclusion might be drawn that the justices declared separate educational facilities *for whatever reason provided* are morally wrong and if supported by tax funds are illegal. Yet on reading carefully the whole opinion, I think the key sentence is the question defined by the Court: "Does segregation of children in public schools *solely* on the basis of race, even though the physical facilities and other 'tangible' factors may be equal, deprive the children of the minority group of equal educational opportunities? We believe that it does." I have italicized the word "solely," as I presume to think it is the essential word. The justices appear to have expressed no view as to whether the pupils in a completely Negro school are deprived of equal educational opportunity if they are not assigned solely because of their race. In short, if one group of children is separated from another group because of the neighborhood in which they live, the fact of this separation is, of and by itself, no evidence of an inequality in education. Whether in fact the facilities and instruction are equal in a 100 per cent white school, a mixed school, and a 100 per cent Negro school in a large city is to be determined by examining the schools, not by appeal to phrases such as *de facto* segregation with the implication that it is to be condemned by all right-thinking people who condemn *de jure* segregation.

In some cities, political leaders have attempted to put pressure on the school authorities to have Negro children attend essentially white schools. In my judgment the cities in which the authorities have yielded to this pressure are on the wrong track. Those which have not done so, like

Chicago, are more likely to make progress in improving Negro education. It is my belief that satisfactory education can be provided in an all-Negro school through the expenditure of more money for needed staff and facilities. Moreover, I believe that any sense of inferiority among the pupils caused by the absence of white children can be largely if not wholly eliminated in two ways: first, in all cities there will be at least some schools that are in fact mixed because of the nature of the neighborhood they serve; second, throughout the city there ought to be an integrated staff of white and Negro teachers and administrators.

To insist that such solutions cannot be acceptable and to assume instead that the schooling of Negroes can be satisfactory only if in each schoolroom there are present some white children is to take an extremely defeatist view of Negro education in the large cities. The proposal to move any appreciable number of white children by bus into what are now Negro schools or to move all the Negro children in a Negro neighborhood into what are now white schools presents a transportation problem that is quite insoluble. An examination of the geography of the Negro and white sections of the large cities makes this evident. If some children are to be transported, the question arises which children and how many. I am not discussing here what seems to me to be a separate question; namely, the crossing of school attendance lines when waves of population movement create overcrowded conditions in one attendance area and vacancies in another. Nor am I justifying the gerrymandering of attendance lines; such a procedure amounts to separating pupils *solely* on the basis of race.

At the elementary school level the issue seems clear. To send young children day after day to distant schools by bus seems out of the question. It must be remembered that unless by the accident of population migration there are empty seats in the predominantly white schools, white chil-

dren would have to be transported to Negro areas in order
to free the necessary space. Clearly a complicated arrangement for moving large groups of young children around a
city for the sake of mixing all the elementary schools is
hardly worth discussing. At the high school level, the
youth are certainly old enough to commute; one complication present in the elementary schools has disappeared.
Still, a great network of transportation would have to be
provided in a number of cities if the goal were to have every
high school a mixed school. I have already noted the problem of determining the proper degree of admixture of white
and Negro children. The more one considers the matter,
the more one is convinced that children should not be
manipulated for the purpose of seating Negro children in
white schools or vice versa. To my mind, the city school
superintendent is right who said he was in the education
business and should not become involved in attempts to
correct the consequences of voluntary segregated housing.

I know the argument is being made that crossing attendance lines should be permissive and without cost to the
city and that the refusal of this right is a psychological blow
to the pride of the members of the Negro race. But the reason for demanding such a privilege is the allegation that
education in an all-Negro school to which pupils are not
assigned *solely* on account of race is inherently inferior.
Once this allegation is granted, the foundation for improving Negro education in the large cities is undermined. Since
I believe the evidence indicates that it is the socio-economic
situation, not the color of the children, which makes the
Negro slum schools so difficult, the real issue is not racial
integration but socio-economic integration.

Put another way, if there is no inherent difference
in potential ability, and if educational opportunity is equal,
the poor achievement of the children in both the Negro
and white slums which I described earlier may be ascribed to
their depressing cultural and socio-economic backgrounds.

One might argue, therefore, that *all* slum schools ought to be integrated with schools in economically favored areas. If the body politic through its school board once sets out on a course of neighborhood desegregation, a good case can be made for transporting *white* children from slum schools to schools in high income residential districts and vice versa.

Much as I admire the comprehensive high school in the town with one high school and see it as an instrument of democracy, it seems impossible for school authorities in a large city to create artificially a series of such schools. If a policy were to be adopted that, as an ideal, every neighborhood school should have a widely heterogeneous school population represented by all socio-economic backgrounds, school administrators would be forced to move children about as though they were pawns on a chessboard.

If good schools can exist only with a heterogeneous student population, one could argue just as logically that state authorities should adjust all school district lines so that the high-income suburban high school would include students from a neighboring depressed area. Another impossible proposal. Antithetical to our free society as I believe *de jure* segregation to be, I think it would be far better for those who are agitating for the deliberate mixing of children to accept *de facto* segregated schools as a consequence of a present housing situation and to work for the improvement of slum schools whether Negro or white. The problems in these schools are far more difficult to solve than in other schools, larger and better staffs should be available, more money is required. It is my firm belief that actions based on the premises I have outlined are in the best interests of the Negro and of the nation. Through the existence of at least some mixed schools, integrated teaching staffs, and increased expenditures in slum schools, I suggest that the education of Negroes in Northern cities can be made satisfactory and their status improved. Another necessary step in upgrading the status of the Negro in the North is to take drastic measures to eliminate racial discrimination by labor unions and employers. This last observation leads me to a consideration of employment and secondary education in the large cities, which is the subject of the next chapter.

# CHAPTER II

## Schools and Jobs in the Big Cities

Among the preoccupations of those concerned with underprivileged areas, one often encounters a great emphasis on the importance of adequate, decent housing. To be sure, the inhabitants in the slums (Negro and white) may be living in shockingly bad and even dangerous dwellings. They may also be living in new housing which is the result of a slum clearance project. I am willing to assume that improving the physical environment improves the lives of the inhabitants. To the extent that increased housing facilities diminish the mobility of the population, they may even have a direct bearing on the problem of education. But I am sure new housing works no miracles. I offer the following hypothesis for professional social workers and sociologists to demolish—namely, that the correlation between desirable social attitudes (including attitudes of youth) and job opportunities is far higher than between the former and housing conditions, as measured by plumbing and heating facilities and space per family.

In preparation for a Conference on Unemployed, Out-of-School Youth in Urban Areas held in May, 1961, a few special studies were conducted in slum areas of large cities to find out what the facts really were with respect to the unemployment of youth in slum neighborhoods. In a slum section composed almost entirely of Negroes in one of our largest cities the following situation was found: A total of 59 per cent of the male youth between the ages of sixteen and twenty-one were out of school and unemployed. They were roaming the streets. Of the boys who graduated from high school 48 per cent were unemployed in contrast to 63 per cent of the boys who had dropped out of school. In short, two thirds of the male dropouts did not have jobs and about half of the high school graduates did not have jobs. In such a situation, the pupil may ask, "Why bother to stay in school when graduation for half the boys opens onto a dead-end street?"

An even worse state of affairs was found in another special study in a different city. In a slum area of 125,000 people, mostly Negro, a sampling of the youth population showed that roughly 70 per cent of the boys and girls ages sixteen to twenty-one were out of school and unemployed. When one considers that the total population in this district is equal to that of a good-sized independent city, the magnitude of the problem is appalling and the challenge to our society is clear.

I do not have to remind the reader that the fate of freedom in the world hangs very much in balance. Our success against the spread of communism in no small measure depends upon the successful operation of our own free society. To my mind, there is no question that a healthy society requires a sound economy and high employment. Communism feeds upon discontented, frustrated, unemployed people. As I write in June, 1961, the unemployment rate nationwide is something over 7 per cent for all age brackets, but unemployment among youth under twenty-one years of age is about 17 per cent, or more than twice the nationwide rate for all workers. These young people are my chief concern, especially when they are pocketed together in large numbers within the confines of the big city slums. What can words like "freedom," "liberty," and "equality of opportunity" mean to these young people? With what kind of zeal and dedication can we expect them to withstand the relentless pressures of communism? How well prepared are they to face the struggle that shows no signs of abating?

I am deeply disturbed by the implications that widespread unemployment among the youth of our big cities has for the future of our society.

Although the causes of juvenile delinquency are complex and there is no one solution, employment opportunities are clearly important. A youth who has dropped out of school and never has had a full-time job is not likely to become a constructive citizen of his community. Quite the contrary. As a frustrated individual he is likely to be anti-social and rebellious, and may well become a juvenile delinquent. The adverse influence of the street is largely a consequence of gangs of such youths, out of school and unemployed. I doubt if anyone familiar with slums would deny that, if all the male youth by some miracle were to find employment, the social climate would change dramatically for the better. Some juvenile delinquents would remain, gangs might not wholly disappear, but the attitude of the neighborhood would alter in such a way as to make more effective the teacher in every classroom.

Unemployment is bad anywhere. Adult unemployment, especially in rural areas, towns, and small cities, is grievous because it usually involves the loss of support for an entire family. In such cases, one might say that solving the unemployment of adults has the top priority. But in the slums of the largest cities, the reverse is true. The great need is for reduction of unemployment of male youth under twenty-one.

Consider for a moment the long-run consequence of persistent failure of underprivileged youth to find work. Leaving aside the human tragedies involved in each individual instance and looking at the matter solely in terms of the welfare of our free society, one sees the special position of the large city slums. The boys brought up in slum neighborhoods, even if they come to the big city from the country as children, are conditioned to street life with all that this life implies. Out of work and out of school once they turn sixteen, these youth behave in ways that may have serious political consequences; similar behavior of youth in smaller cities would be far less serious. It is a matter of geography in the last analysis. Three factors are significant: first, group size (the larger the group, the more dangerous); second, the density of the population (the number of frustrated youth per block); third, the isolation of the inhabitants from other kinds of people and other sorts of streets and houses.

If one compares the slum areas in the largest cities with similar districts in small cities, the difference with respect to these three factors is evident. The youth in the big city slums dwell in a mammoth social complex. The surrounding city extends for many blocks. The business and industrial areas hem in the impoverished youth. In the case of the Negro, added to all the negative influences of a slum is the absence of any evidence that there is a pathway out. In spite of the high mobility of the family unit, or perhaps because of it, a tone is set by constant talk and the prevailing attitude of the older people. The tone is not one to encourage education or stimulate ambition. One often finds a vicious circle of lack of jobs and lack of ambition; one leads to the other. It is my contention that the circle must be broken both by upgrading the educational and vocational aspirations of slum youth and, even more important, by finding employment opportunity for them, particularly for high school graduates. It does no good whatever to prepare boys and girls for nonexistent jobs.

The difference between the Negro slum of today and the slums of the Northern seaport cities of sixty years ago is a difference that deserves attention. The worries I have expressed about the continuation of present conditions may appear to be neutralized by contemplating the record of the past. Big cities have always had slums. In the United States in the past it was possible for people to raise themselves by their own bootstraps in the course of a generation. Why be alarmed about the present situation? Such a complacent projection of the past into the obscure future is fallacious for several reasons. First and foremost is the fact that in the past most of the inhabitants of slums were recently arrived white foreign immigrants. They knew that their predecessors for generations had worked their way out of poverty in the cities. They were convinced that they could do likewise. The almost complete lack of such conviction—a consequence of the tragic story of the Negro in the United States—is the outstanding characteristic of youth in the Negro slum. Secondly, a foreign immigrant came from an impoverished but stable society, for the most part a peasant society with its own ancient mores. The pride of family and often strong church connections were social cement that kept the slums from being complete social jungles in spite of the fact that the dwelling conditions were often as bad as they are today. Lastly, for most of the period of our history labor shortages rather than labor surpluses were characteristic of our economy. Particularly, unskilled laborers were in demand. When this was not so, namely, in the depression years, organized society had to step in on a large scale to bolster the tottering social structure. Today automation has affected the employment scene; there is much less demand for unskilled labor. Racial discrimination makes unemployment chronic for the Negro male, North and South. In short, neither in terms of the kinds of people involved nor in terms of the economic and social setting is there much resemblance between the poor city districts of 1900 and those which are the sore spots of our modern cities.

What was especially disturbing to me in my visits to the largest cities was the discovery that the employment of youth is literally nobody's affair. To be sure, there are groups concerned with various aspects of the problem, but no single agency in any of the cities has the data as to the unemployment picture in that city. There is little up-to-date information about youth unemployment even city-wide and only the estimate of school people about the slum neighborhoods. Seldom are figures available to distinguish between the unemployed who are high school graduates and those who have dropped out of school before completing the twelfth grade. Most important, it is not possible to say with any accuracy how the unemployed youth are distributed among various neighborhoods. At the beginning of this chapter I cited special studies that were undertaken to ascertain the extent of unemployment among out-of-school youth in slum neighborhoods. These studies corroborated my guess that the situation was bad. There is a great need for reliable information of this sort. Until public opinion demands that the employment of youth be looked at with a microscope, so to speak, neighborhood by neighborhood, we are unlikely to rectify what may be a great hidden danger.

One gets just so far with a discussion of the urban problem and unemployment and then runs into a set of roadblocks set up by the leaders of the Negro communities and their friends. I refer to the fact that it is considered illiberal, if not reactionary, to use the phrase I have been using, "Negro slum." Indeed, it is difficult if not impossible to get statistics about school enrollment and employment in terms of the categories white and Negro. I understand the reasons for the erection of this roadblock, but I suggest that in the interest of the Negroes themselves it is time to remove it. The urban problem is in part a Negro problem. We do not facilitate its solution by trying to find phrases to hide this fact. And it is largely a Negro problem in the North because of the discrimination practiced quietly but extensively by employers and by labor unions. In an effort to overcome this unjust and nationally dangerous discrimination, Negro leaders and their friends have placed a taboo on the use of the word "Negro." I think this has proved to be a great mistake. How can we improve a situation if we are deprived by terminology from knowing what the situation really is?

Whereas the problems of Negro education are no different from those of all underprivileged socio-economic groups, the problems of Negro employment are distinctly different. The enforcement of antidiscrimination laws has proved a most difficult undertaking. It is generally agreed that only the projects which are supported by public funds can really be operated on a truly nondiscriminatory basis. Therefore because of the urgency of the situation, I think it is necessary for Congress to appropriate funds for public work programs to alleviate unemployment among youth of sixteen to twenty-one in the large cities. I estimate that roughly 300,000 jobs are needed.

As I write, the President has submitted to Congress a draft of a Youth Employment Opportunities Act of 1961. This small pilot program for youth ages 16–21 has three parts. The first is on-the-job training programs run by local employers, unions, and educational institutions and subsidized by federal funds. This program would be largely for school dropouts. The second approach involves public service employment in schools, hospitals, parks, and other publicly operated facilities. Federal subsidies are involved here as well. The third approach is similar to the Civilian Conservation Corps of depression days. Youths would live in camps, receive education and training, and work on conservation and forest projects. I question the relevance of the CCC proposal to the problem of unemployed youth in the large cities. What is needed are jobs in the big cities on a non-discriminatory basis. Two of the three proposals appear to be directly applicable to the situation I have been discussing. But they would be effective only if a non-discriminatory provision is included and enforced.

## The Role of the Schools

At the outset I must record an educational heresy, or rather support a proposition that many will accept as self-evident but that some professors of the liberal arts will denounce as dangerously heretical. *I submit that in a heavily urbanized and industrialized free society the educational experiences of youth should fit their subsequent employment.* There should be a smooth transition from full-time schooling to a full-time job, whether that transition be after grade 10 or after graduation from high school, college, or university.

This is an ideal situation admittedly, and one which is at present approached only in the learned professions and in a few instances the occupations for which undergraduate courses provide the necessary training. In the case of the learned professions, those in charge of the last stage in the educational journey—the professors of law, of medicine, and those who direct the research of candidates for the Ph.D.—have usually a sense of responsibility for their students based on their own passionate interest in promoting the best interests of their profession. Graduates of some undergraduate professional courses in some institutions are also often assisted in finding employment. Engineering is perhaps the best example. With the present shortage of teachers, professors of education have no difficulty in finding jobs for their students. While the universities or colleges do not accept responsibility for the placement of their graduates, many, if not all, spend time and money in helping the young man or woman to find a job. In many cases the subsequent career is followed with interest, and assistance is provided in re-employment. Sixty years ago the situation was very different. Concern with placement of college and university graduates was a product of the depression years. The change, I believe, has been important and in the best interests of both the individual and society. For the college graduate who has received a general or liberal education without majoring in a professional or semi-professional field, many difficulties of finding a suitable job will remain. Still, by and large, one can say at the college and university level a considerable fraction of the youth involved make a smooth transition from education to a job.

When we examine the situation at the high school level, we find quite a different state of affairs. Although half or more of the graduates of many high schools seek employment immediately on graduation, only in a few cities does one find an effective placement service. I make this statement without intending any reproach to either social agencies, employment offices, or to guidance officers. The obligations of the school should not end when the student either drops out of school or graduates. At that point the cumulative record folder concerning a student's educational career is usually brought to an end. It should not be. To my mind, *guidance officers, especially in the large cities, ought to be given the responsibility for following the post-high school careers of youth from the time they leave school until they are twenty-one years of age.* Since compulsory attendance usually ends at age sixteen, this means responsibility for the guidance of youth ages sixteen to twenty-one who are out of school and either employed or unemployed. This expansion of the school's function will cost money and will mean additional staff—at least a doubling of the guidance staff in most of the large cities. But the expense is necessary, for vocational and educational guidance must be a continuing process to help assure a smooth transition from school to the world of work. The present abrupt break between the two is unfortunate. What I have in mind suggests, of course, a much closer relationship than now exists among the schools, employers, and labor unions, as well as social agencies and employment offices.

In a few school districts one finds a link between school and job. In those vocational programs organized with Smith–Hughes money, there may be a close tie between the labor union and a local employer on the one hand and the vocational teacher on the other. In these cases a graduate may enter directly into an apprentice program, saving a year because of his vocational courses in grades 11 and 12. The apprentice program will involve further education on a part-time basis, usually at night, perhaps using some of the same equipment of the high school. These opportunities are to be found in certain cities in such crafts as auto mechanics, carpentry, drafting, electrical work, tool-and-die work, and sheet-metal work.

Formally organized vocational programs supported by federal funds allow high school students to gain experience in a field of work which is likely to lead to a full-time job on graduation. The "diversified occupations" program is a part-time trade-preparatory program conducted over two school years on a cooperative basis between the school and local industrial and business employers. The "distributive education" program operates in a similar way, with arrangements between the school and employers in merchandising fields. In both cases the student attends school half-time and works in a regular job the other half. He receives remuneration for his work. In a few places cooperative programs between schools and employers in clerical work have shown the same possibilities for allowing the student, while still in school, to develop skills which are immediately marketable upon graduation.

Adult education courses, work-study programs of various sorts—these are all evidence of a continuing interest of the schools in furthering educational opportunities for out-of-school youth. In general, however, it may be said that when a boy or a girl leaves the high school, the school authorities play little or no part in the decision of what happens next. If the student drops out of high school, the break with the school is even more complete. When there is employment opportunity for youth, this arrangement—or lack of arrangement—works out quite well. Indeed, in some periods of our history and in some neighborhoods the job opportunities have been so good that undoubtedly a great many boys who were potential members of the professions quit school at an early age and went to work. Statistically this has represented a loss to the nation, although one must admit that in an individual case the decision in retrospect may have been a wise one. I make no attempt to measure the enduring satisfaction and material well-being of a man who went to work on graduation from high school and was highly successful in the business which he entered. He may or may not be "better off" than his classmate who went on to a college and professional school. But in the next decades the nation needs to educate for the professions all the potential professional talent.

In a later chapter dealing with the suburban school, I shall discuss the importance of arranging a program for the academically talented and highly gifted youth in any high school where he is found. In the Negro neighborhoods and also to some extent in the mixed neighborhoods the problem may be one of identification and motivation. High motivation towards higher education must start early enough so that by the time the boy or girl reaches grade 9 he or she has at least developed those basic skills which are essential for academic work. Undoubtedly far more can be done in the lower grades in this regard in the Negro schools. However, the teacher can only go so far if the attitude of the community and the family is anti-intellectual. And the fact remains that there are today few shining examples of Negroes in positions of intellectual leadership. This is not due to any policy of discrimination on the part of the Northern universities. Quite the contrary, as I can testify from personal experience as a former university president. Rather we see here another vicious circle.

The absence of successful Negroes in the world of scholarship and science has tended to tamp down enthusiasm among Negro youth for academic careers. I believe the situation is improving, but the success stories need to be heavily publicized. Here again we run into the roadblock that Negroes do not like to be designated as Negroes in the press. How can the vicious circle be broken? This is a problem to which leaders of opinion, both Negro and white, should devote far more attention. It is at least as important as the more dramatic attempts to break down barriers of inequality in the South.

## Vocational Education

I should like to underline four points I made in my first report with respect to vocational education. First and foremost, vocational courses should not replace courses which are essential parts of the required academic program for graduation. Second, vocational courses should be provided in grades 11 and 12 and not require more than half the student's time in those years; however, for slow learners and prospective dropouts these courses ought to begin earlier. Third, the significance of the vocational courses is that those enrolled are keenly interested in the work; they realize the relevance of what they are learning to their future careers, and this sense of purpose is carried over to the academic courses which they are studying at the same time. Fourth, the type of vocational training programs should be related to the employment opportunities in the general locality. This last point is important because if high school pupils are aware that few, if any, graduates who have chosen a certain vocational program have obtained a job as a consequence of the training, the whole idea of relevance disappears. Vocational training which holds no hope that the skill developed will be in fact a marketable skill becomes just another school "chore" for those whose interest in their studies has begun to falter. Those who, because of population mobility and the reputed desire of employers to train their own employees, would limit vocational education to general rather than specific skills ought to bear in mind the importance of motivation in any kind of school experience.

I have been using the word "vocational" as a layman would at first sight think it should be used. I intend to include under the term all the practical courses open to boys and girls. These courses develop skills other than those we think of when we use the adjective "academic." Practically all of these practical skills are of such a nature that a degree of mastery can be obtained in high school sufficient to enable the youth to get a job at once on the basis of the skill. They are in this sense skills marketable immediately on graduation from high school. To be sure, in tool-and-die work and in the building trades, the first job must be often on an apprentice basis, but two years of half-time vocational training enables the young man thus to anticipate one year of apprentice status. Similarly, a girl who graduates with a good working knowledge of stenography and the use of clerical machines and who is able to get a job at once may wish to improve her skill and knowledge by a year or two of further study in a community college or secretarial school. Of course, it can be argued that an ability to write English correctly and with some degree of elegance is a marketable skill. So, too, is the mathematical competence of a college graduate who has majored in mathematics. In a sense almost all high school and college courses could be considered as vocational to the extent that later in life the student in his vocation (which may be a profession) will be called upon to use some of the skills developed and the competence obtained. In spite of the shading of one type of course into another, I believe it is useful to talk about vocational courses as apart from academic courses. Perhaps a course in typewriting might be regarded as the exception which proves the rule. Today many college bound students try to take a course in personal typing, as they feel a certain degree of mastery of this skill is almost essential for one who proposes to do academic work in college and a professional school.

Most of our largest cities have one or more separate vocational or technical high schools. In this respect, public education in the large cities differs from education in the smaller cities and consolidated school districts. The neighborhood high schools are not, strictly speaking, comprehensive schools, because some of the boys and girls may be attending a vocational or technical high school instead of the local school. Indeed, one school superintendent in a large city objects to the use of the term comprehensive high school for the senior high schools in his city, because these schools do not offer strictly vocational programs. He prefers to designate such schools as "general" high schools. The suburban high school, it is worth noting, also is not a widely comprehensive high school because of the absence of vocational programs. The reason is that there is a lack of interest on the part of the community. Therefore employment and education in all the schools in a metropolitan area are related in different ways from those which are characteristic of the comprehensive high school described in my first report.

The separate vocational or technical high schools in the large cities must be reckoned as permanent institutions. By and large their programs are satisfactorily connected both to the employment situation and to the realities of the apprentice system. It is not often realized to what degree certain trades are in many communities closed areas of employment, except for a lucky few. One has to talk confidentially with some of the directors of vocational high schools to realize that a boy cannot just say, "I want to be a plumber," and then, by doing good work, find a job. It is far more difficult in many communities to obtain admission to an apprentice program which involves union approval than to get into the most selective medical school in the nation. Two stories will illustrate what I have in mind. One vocational instructor in a city vocational school, speaking of his course in a certain field, said he had no difficulty placing all students in jobs *outside* of the city. In the city, he said, the waiting list for those who want to join the union is so long that unless a boy has an inside track he can't get in. In a far distant part of the United States, I was talking to an instructor about a boy who in the twelfth grade was doing special work. "What does he have in mind to do when he graduates?" "Oh, he'll be a plumber," came the answer. "But isn't it almost impossible to get into the union?" I asked. "He'll have no difficulty," I was told. "He has very good connections."

In my view, there should be a school which offers significant vocational programs for boys within easy reach of every family in a city. Ideally these schools should be so located that one or more should be in the area where demand for practical courses is at the highest.

An excellent example of a successful location of a new vocational high school is the Dunbar Vocational High School in Chicago. Located in a bad slum area now undergoing redevelopment, this school and its program are especially tailored to the vocational aims of its students. Hardly a window has been broken since Dunbar first was opened (and vandalism in schools is a major problem in many slum areas). I discovered in the course of a visit there that almost all the pupils were Negroes. They were learning trades as diverse as shoe repairing, bricklaying, carpentry, cabinet making, auto mechanics, and airplane mechanics. The physical facilities at Dunbar are impressive, but more impressive is the attitude of the pupils. Motivation is good and the students take obvious pride in their work. The academic side of the program is conducted on a high level

—high enough so that if a graduate decides he wishes to attend college he may do so. Every year, a few Dunbar graduates do go on to a liberal arts college, but this is not the primary purpose of the school. Most graduates go directly into industry. The Dunbar school, to my mind, approaches the ideal in vocational education.

Having said all this in favor of vocational programs, I must record my strong feeling that the whole subject of vocational education, and especially of separate federal and state support, requires a thorough reappraisal. I know that some of the programs in some schools have long since ceased to be realistic. I know that in some states a self-perpetuating bureaucracy has gained control. I know that the agricultural courses, in particular, require overhauling and that new areas should be explored.

## Vocational Work in the General High School

The separate vocational schools in the large city enroll at best but a very small fraction of the youth. What sort of high school program is left for those average students who, for one reason or another, cannot attend the separate vocational school? (This group might include, for example, those who find it difficult to attend a specialized school because it is in a distant part of the city.)

In the higher-income residential areas, there may be practically no demand for programs to develop marketable skills. On the other hand, in those districts where parents are likely to be more realistic about their children and where there is a clear recognition that education beyond the high school is not necessarily a good idea for all, the demand for practical courses is certain to be present. The general high school can offer such courses for girls (stenography and clerical machines, home economics, for example). Girls with clerical and stenographic skills are in high demand in the large cities. The problem comes with the boys. Those male pupils who might like to develop a manual skill have no recourse except to continue their work in industrial arts, in my opinion all too often an unsatisfactory substitute for a vocational course.

What can be done in the general high school to improve the situation for boys? An auto mechanics shop is often an extremely worthwhile addition to a school program. In charge of a good mechanic (*not* the usual type of industrial arts teacher who is a college graduate) the instruction can be very practical. Most boys today with any liking for tools enjoy this type of work. The degree of intensity and the amount of time devoted will determine the competence of those who finish grade 12. Some graduates will be well on the way to becoming auto mechanics; others will not have reached this level but will have developed a skill with tools that is clearly related to many job opportunities. Why not have such a shop in every general high school and have the instructors part of the vocational staff of the entire city, their efforts coordinated by someone on the vocational high school staff? If this idea has merit, why might not a similar development take place with electronics shops? The clearing house for the employment of those thus trained in the general high school shops would be the vocational high school.

I recognize at once an objection to this scheme which springs from our present complicated pattern of teacher certificates. Academic teachers object to having as colleagues practical electricians or auto mechanics without college degrees. Hence regulations have been written in some states which would hamper the school board in employing the skilled mechanic or electrician except in clearly labeled vocational programs. And, too, programs with this label run into the state bureaucracy of the vocational people. However, if the state vocational authorities will agree, vocational programs can be distributed among the general high schools of a large city, as is being done in Detroit. In that city the aim is to have at least a few vocational programs in virtually every school, with the hope that this kind of program will correspond to the ambitions of many parents and students in the neighborhood.

## The Slow Learner and the High School Dropout

By and large, the opportunities opened by these programs would be for the average or better-than-average student. By this I mean students who in grade 9 are not reading below the eighth-grade level and whose scholastic aptitude puts them in the upper 60 to 70 per cent of the ninth-grade population on a national basis. In some of the schools in the slums, however, one finds today an incredibly large percentage of pupils who may be properly designated as slow and very-slow learners. The outstanding characteristic of this group which can be easily determined is an extremely low reading level. What type of studies in the higher grades should be provided for such a child, remembering the nature of the neighborhood involved? In general terms, one may answer the question I have just raised by prescribing a general education and a vocational education, both of which should be geared to the pupil's abilities and his desires. Above all, the total school experience should be such, if possible, to anchor the boy's or girl's interest in the school and in improving his or her capacity through education.

Under present employment circumstances, it does seem that a high school diploma is an asset for virtually all students. However, realistically one must face the fact that not all will remain in school long enough to graduate. For the many slow learners, it may actually be worse to stay in school and endure constant academic frustration than to leave school and to find a satisfying job, if such a job can be found. Boys in this group have much more difficulty finding a job than girls. I am not impressed by the holding power of a school as a criterion of its quality, but neither am I impressed by the argument that a boy who fails to get along in school ought to drop out. It all depends. The situation in which a boy drops out of school only to walk the streets is quite different from the situation in which a boy drops out and finds satisfactory employment. Full-time schooling for certain youths through grade 12 may be good or bad, depending upon the employment picture.

The recent trend in employment opportunities indicates that fewer and fewer completely unskilled workers will be able to obtain jobs in the decade ahead. Employers will want skilled workers. If present trends continue, professional workers will be in heavy demand. White collar jobs will grow at a more rapid rate than blue collar jobs, and it is quite clear that except for one area of employment there will be little demand for unskilled workers—the slow learners and high school dropouts who constitute a major problem in large city slums. The one area of employment that would seem to offer hope for these students is the service occupations. The growth in the number of service workers in the past ten years was second only to the growth in the number of professional workers. These service occupations are especially important in the economy of the large cities—all the jobs ranging from hotel bellboys to messengers to laundry operatives. Therefore I think it would be worthwhile for the schools to investigate the many possibilities that may exist with respect to work-experience programs for slow learners in these trades followed by full-time employment on jobs that require little in the way of developed skills. The cooperation of local industries—hotels, for instance—is a necessity, and one of my purposes here is to jolt conscientious citizens into an awareness of the need for their help in solving this problem.

There is a real difficulty in trying to find suitable vocational tasks for slow learners. Philadelphia has recently introduced in a few schools so-called occupational practice shops. The emphasis in these shops is the same as in all vocational programs, namely, to develop marketable skills. In this case, however, since the pupils have extremely low academic ability and achieve below their grade placement, relatively simple types of manual skills are being developed. Many in these courses do not stay through the four years but leave school after two years with a certificate attesting to the particular skill developed. Because the students are extremely unlikely to be able to finish four years of high school, the vocational emphasis quite properly starts in grade 9 and is not postponed until grade 11 as would be the case in a typical widely comprehensive high school. The significance of the program is the frank recognition that there are many potential dropouts in certain neighborhoods and that to help these youths fit into the employment picture some practical courses of a simple type must be available in grades 9 and 10.

In Detroit a "job upgrading program" is designed to help exactly the same type of youth who in Philadelphia is guided into the occupational practice shops. In Detroit, however, the upgrading centers operate independently of the regular curriculum of a high school, though they are located in a school building. A counselor is available for these unemployed out-of-school pupils who wish to find employment. Many are taking advantage of the opportunities offered and the number of centers is being expanded. The youth spends the morning with the counselor and is part of a group of some twenty-five to thirty boys and girls. For many the assistance rendered may involve such simple matters as learning how to dress and be groomed, how to shake hands and greet a prospective employer, how to complete job applications. Enrollment in classes in the regular high school curriculum may be the answer for some. The main effort, however, is to assist these young people in obtaining employment. To this end, after about six weeks' attendance at the center, six weeks of supervised work in private industry or in a public agency may follow. Contact is maintained with the state employment agency, and those who attend the centers are shown how to seek employment through this agency and through other means.

A new Urban Service Corps providing public employment for unemployed youth in Detroit is another promising development. New York City has recently begun a Youth Employment Service (YES). As worthwhile as I think all these efforts are, I would be less than frank if I did not say that the magnitude of the task dwarfs the efforts of the dedicated people running these and similar programs. Surely, they are a step in the right direction, but not a solution. I am not sure that educators anywhere have found a solution to the problem of the kind of education suitable for a slow learner through twelve years of schooling. The difficulties are aggravated in the large cities. Therefore, at this point I should like to turn the reader's attention in the next chapter to some of the important matters with respect to the organization and management of public education in our large urban centers.

# CHAPTER III

## Problems of Curriculum and Organization

*Diversity and Size*

The purpose of this chapter is to identify some of the problems faced in large cities in connection with the curriculum and the structure and organization of the schools. Two factors combine to make the difficulties especially acute. One is a fact I have stressed before: Large cities comprise many diverse neighborhoods. In this volume I am contrasting the high-income suburbs with the low-income slum areas of the cities. The same contrast can be found within many of the cities themselves. The nature of the tasks presented to school administrators and teachers varies incredibly from one neighborhood to another. As the problems vary, so the solutions vary, and no set of administrative decisions in the central office of a district that embraces these diverse communities can have validity for all.

The second factor that complicates the public school situation in the large cities is the magnitude of the task. New York City best illustrates what is involved. With an annual budget of about $500 million, it is the largest school district in the United States, and its more than 800 schools enroll close to 1 million pupils. There are only four cities that individually have total populations that exceed New York City's public school enrollment—Chicago, Los Angeles, Philadelphia, and Detroit. Even more impressive is the fact that the public school enrollment in New York City is greater than that found in each of thirty-nine states and greater than the combined enrollments of nine states: Vermont, New Hampshire, Rhode Island, Alaska, Delaware, Montana, Wyoming, North Dakota, and South Dakota. In each of these nine states one usually finds a chief state school officer at the head of a state department of education and a state board of education at the top of a hierarchical structure that includes innumerable local school boards and locally appointed administrators in the many districts within the state. In fact, in these nine states there are roughly 6000 local school districts. Imagine the magnitude of the task of the New York City superintendent in contrast to that of the administrative officer in each of these 6000 districts!

One must bear in mind when discussing the structure of school systems the fact that school districts and municipalities are not always coterminous. Moreover, the boundaries of a school district are subject to state policy as set forth in state legislation. School board members, even though they may be elected locally, are officials whose duties are prescribed by the state. In short, public school districts are creations of the state, not of local municipalities. Consequently one finds throughout the nation school districts of every size and description and school boards with a great variety of financial powers. For example, among the forty largest school districts in the nation in terms of enrollment there are six districts organized on a county basis, all reflecting the importance of county government in the South. One of the ten largest districts in the nation, for instance, is Dade County, Florida, which encompasses not only Miami but suburban and rural areas outside the city limits. The diversity in the neighborhoods served in such a system is certainly as marked as that found in any large city system. Numbered also among the ten largest districts is the State of Hawaii, the only truly state system in the nation. In Hawaii there are no local districts or local school boards and superintendents; school revenues and expenditures are determined at the state level, as are curriculum matters and the hiring and placement of teachers.

At all events, in the rest of this chapter I shall speak of the large cities, but one should remember that my remarks apply equally to Hawaii and the districts organized on a county basis. In order of size of enrollment the ten largest school districts in the country are:

| District | Public school enrollment | Total population (1960 Census) |
|---|---|---|
| 1. New York, N.Y. | 958,100 | 7,781,984 |
| 2. Los Angeles, Calif. | 537,971 | 2,479,015 |
| 3. Chicago, Ill. | 452,080 | 3,550,404 |
| 4. Detroit, Mich. | 282,483 | 1,670,144 |
| 5. Philadelphia, Pa. | 235,037 | 2,002,512 |
| 6. Baltimore, Md. | 163,000 | 939,024 |
| 7. Houston, Texas | 149,939 | 938,219 |
| 8. Dade County, Fla. | 146,206 | 935,047 |
| 9. State of Hawaii | 133,535 | 632,772 |
| 10. Cleveland, Ohio | 127,816 | 876,050 |

The presence of diverse communities within a large district causes many problems with respect to curriculum and staffing. Latitude must be granted to the schools by the central office for curricular and instructional innovation to meet local needs. It is essential at the secondary level when differentiated programs in the form of elective subjects are taken, but it is equally important at the elementary level as well. An elementary syllabus mandated for all schools by the central office is likely to frustrate slow children, in particular those in such deprived areas as the big city Negro slums, and fail to challenge the children in the suburban-type neighborhood. The time necessary for work on basic skills will vary considerably from one school to another. In an elementary school in a slum area a major fraction of the school day ought to be devoted to reading skills. I am convinced that a common denominator among unsuccessful school children who later become dropouts and perhaps juvenile delinquents is the failure to develop reading skills. Once these pupils reach the junior high school, it may well be too late to salvage them.

A number of highly constructive programs designed to help the very-slow reader are now under way in several cities. At this point, I should like to discuss a few of these in some detail.

## The Reading Problem

In St. Louis, school administrators feel that pupils with reading difficulties ought to be caught early, certainly prior to the fourth grade. In the first three grades learning to read is perhaps the major occupation of the pupil. Commencing in about grade 4, reading becomes a tool for learning. Consequently pupils who have not sufficiently mastered reading skills have ever-increasing difficulty with textbooks in different subject areas. In 1953 the St. Louis elementary schools organized special groups called "Rooms of Twenty." In these groups were placed third-grade pupils who showed that they would have difficulty in the fourth grade. Especially competent teachers were assigned to these rooms and were given a free hand to develop skills in reading, spelling, oral and written language, handwriting, and arithmetic. Studies show substantial progress, and, more important, pupils in these special classes more than hold their own in later schoolwork after a maximum of one year in the special class.

For those whose reading difficulties are even more acute in grades 4 through 6, there are five reading clinics in the city. I was highly impressed with what I saw in these reading clinics. Expensive individual tests of scholastic aptitude are given to these pupils to identify those whose ability may have been masked by reading difficulties on the group paper-and-pencil tests. Group tests measure reading

ability as much as any single factor; therefore for these
pupils it is desirable to have a measure of their aptitude which is not affected by their reading skill. A pupil
who scores low on both a group test and an individual
test may not be expected to gain much despite extra instruction at the reading clinic, whereas a pupil who scores
high on the individual test may progress considerably. The
administrators of the program believe that even the slow-
est readers, leaving aside the mentally retarded, can be
brought up to at least the sixth-grade level. This means the
ability to read with comprehension the front page of a
newspaper or, more specifically, the Gettysburg Address,
at the rate of about 200 words a minute. Children attend these reading clinics for not more than two years,
two or three times a week, while they continue to attend
the elementary school. Finally, an important aspect of these
reading clinics is that they are excellent in-service training
centers for upgrading regular elementary teachers.

Whereas St. Louis has placed great emphasis upon
reading skills in the elementary schools, New York City
is now attacking reading at both the elementary and
junior high school level. The seven-period day in New
York City junior high schools allows room for flexibility,
which in turn means that individual schools can adapt their
program within limits to suit local needs. The junior high
school schedule allots what are called optional periods during the week. In some schools foreign-language instruction, or extra science, or algebra, will be given to bright
pupils in these periods; in other schools these periods are
used mainly for remedial purposes. Many pupils take as
many as ten periods a week of English and remedial reading. A few may take even more remedial reading, as time
is taken from other subjects.

These optional periods are clearly a useful device for
curriculum purposes. But as an illustration of what can happen in a large city system, there is a three-year sequence of

group guidance courses in New York City junior high schools. I can see obvious advantages of such a sequence in slum-area schools, especially in regard to vocational counseling for pupils who may never go beyond grade 9. In such schools, also, there may indeed be a place for some kind of certificate and graduation ceremony at the end of grade 9. In short, these schools may be exceptions to certain of my recommendations in my junior high report, in which I criticized ninth-grade graduation ceremonies and expressed disfavor toward group guidance. In other words, what is good in one school may not be good in another.

Actually, the reading-upgrading program in New York junior high schools has many separate facets. First, there are roughly 135 full-time remedial reading teachers in approximately eighty-five schools. Second, there are the extra periods allotted for instruction, as many as ten per week. Third, and very important from my point of view, is a team project designed for in-service teacher training. The purpose is to improve the teaching of reading in all subject areas, not just English. Seven teams of three expert teachers each go into the schools—one team to a school—for ten weeks and conduct demonstration classes for the teachers. My staff was very much impressed with what they saw. A fourth step may well raise some eyebrows among some professors of education. It is a new and rigorous promotional policy that sets definite standards for pupils to meet, including passing grades, reading proficiency, and satisfactory attendance and behavior.

A final note to the general problem of teaching reading. I have been intrigued with the charge that the so-called "classics" of English and American literature have been rewritten into simpler form for public school children, the implication being that children in the schools today cannot read as well as their predecessors. I think the critics of this innovation are misinformed. The reason for the procedure is simple. There are very few elementary reading materials of mature enough content for adolescent youth who have difficulty with reading—the same youth who would not have been in school fifty years ago. These rewritten classics are specifically for those youth only; they are not written for school children in general. In San Diego I visited a special classroom of very difficult youngsters, including some dropouts who came back to school on a part-time basis. Many of these pupils, sixteen and older, were reading at the third and fourth grade level, but they were interested in what they were reading because the content was mature enough. To my mind, there is little question that these pupils gained more from these simplified classics than they would have from reading comic books or other books written for young children.

## Special Programs for Slum Schools

I might end this brief discussion of elementary and junior high education in the large cities by referring to several projects for improving education in slum schools.

The magnitude of the problem in slum areas is such that in the past few years fourteen of the largest cities have banded together in hopes of attacking the blight that is common to them all. Their joint effort has been generously underwritten by the Ford Foundation under the title of the Great Cities Gray Areas School Improvement Program. "Gray" area projects are now underway in Cleveland, Chicago, Detroit, Milwaukee, Philadelphia, Pittsburgh, and St. Louis. In each of these seven cities a concentrated attack is being made upon a particular aspect of the school problem in slum areas. Included among the projects are such diverse programs as remedial-reading clinics, the establishment of special orientation centers for newly arrived in-migrants from the South who often lack evidence of any educational background, nongraded programs for overaged pupils, and special school-community coordinating teams to integrate efforts of teachers, students, parents, and employers and labor organizations as well as social agencies. Common to all the projects appears to be a direct concern with enlisting community support and motivation for better education in addition to upgrading the instructional program, especially in reading. All these projects represent, to my mind, promising steps to be watched with great interest.

Among the interesting attempts to improve the schooling of slum children is the "Higher Horizons" project in New York. Though it is too early to make a final assessment, results already obtained are encouraging. In 1956 a demonstration guidance project was launched in one Manhattan junior high school where the enrollment was 45 per cent Negro and 40 per cent Puerto Rican. This was an attempt to uncover and encourage talent among slum-area children whose motivation toward education was poor. The aim was to instill within bright children a desire to continue their education and to go to college. Children were chosen in grade 7 on the basis of intelligence, reading and arithmetic tests, and teacher judgment. Counselors were assigned at the ratio of 1 to 250 pupils. A part-time psychologist and part-time social worker were added to the staff, as well as extra teachers. Cultural enrichment was provided in the form of trips to concerts, museums, colleges, plays. Startling improvements on test scores and reduction in behavior problems led in 1959 to the expansion of the project to a number of other schools under the title "Higher Horizons." Both elementary and junior high schools are involved, and though the focus is still on uncovering talent, there is a concern for motivating all the slum children involved.

In connection with an altogether different problem, New York City has what are called "600" schools. These are for disturbed and maladjusted youth unable to get along in the local neighborhood schools. The "600" schools

are not designed to be punitive or custodial but attempt to
rehabilitate these youngsters from chaotic homes and neighborhoods. One characteristic common to these youth is the
inability to read, and remedial reading is high on the agenda.

Another interesting approach to slum school problems
is the Banneker program in St. Louis. This effort had its
origins when a director of elementary education undertook
a general uplifting program for his group of some nine-
teen schools that served a very depressed area populated
mostly by Negroes. Whereas Higher Horizons is aimed
especially at bright children, the Banneker program is aimed
at all children. The academic level of the children in the
Banneker schools was extremely low. Scores on group I.Q.
or scholastic aptitude tests were also low. The elementary
director believed that any program designed to improve this
situation must involve the school principals, the teachers,
the students, and the parents. The basic objective was the
motivation of all concerned. School personnel, aware that
low I.Q. scores meant a prediction of little scholastic success, were urged to forget these scores, as they were urged
to forget race, past failures, and socio-economic status. The
urge to succeed was what had to be developed. Very important was a series of meetings with parents in each
school district to stimulate their interest in their children's
education. There was an aggressive effort to tie closer the
bond between the community and the school. Careful
charts and statistics were kept, and the results claimed were
astonishing.

There are several questions one could raise about
what I have just reported, the most important of which is
perhaps whether this dynamism can be maintained with
the novelty gone. There is, furthermore, the very interesting question of the extent to which motivation can overcome lack of developed ability as tested by scholastic aptitude tests. In other words, how valid are the usual aptitude

or intelligence tests for long range predictions when used in Negro slum schools?

There are other questions as well. As I have indicated earlier, it is not fashionable to identify slums or Negroes. Without such identification, one can easily come to a conclusion that is exactly contrary to one of the main points of this volume—that schools must differ in order to serve specific communities. One is likely to say that all schools should offer Latin, for example. A school without Latin is said to be inferior to schools with Latin teachers. A statement like this is nonsense, if, in fact, the school without Latin teachers has what it should have in the way of remedial reading teachers, guidance personnel, and perhaps social workers. Unfortunately prestige gets mixed into education at every turn. I know that there are schools where Negroes who have difficulty reading English are taking Latin. This is a pathetic situation. Standards are low, as they are in somewhat analogous situations in some suburban schools where parents insist their children take certain academic subjects when they have little or no ability. This is negative education, a waste of time and energy by all concerned.

## Ability Grouping and Tracks

Another problem complicates the situation. If one ignores tests of scholastic aptitude and past achievement, what happens in a racially mixed school with respect to ability grouping? Obviously, without a basis on which to group, no grouping takes place. On the other hand, if one groups by ability, using several different criteria, one is likely to come up with *de facto* segregated classes. This is a very real problem in some schools, especially junior and senior high schools, which, because they draw from a larger attendance area, are likely to be more heterogeneous than

local neighborhood elementary schools. If one has a school
which is practically all-Negro or all-white, the problem is
not so prevalent; it occurs when children from these homogeneous neighborhood schools are brought together.
Some principals publicly say they do not approve of ability
grouping when privately they admit they are afraid of
pressures from outside the school if they did group according to the abilities of the pupils.

My feeling is that in the best interests of all students,
there should be ability grouping in grades 7 through 12 in
such subjects as English, social studies, mathematics, and
science. In short, my recommendation in both my senior
high report and my junior high report still stands. In these
subjects there ought to be subject-by-subject grouping in
three groups—fairly small top and bottom groups and a
large middle group. Such an arrangement may well isolate Negroes in some schools in the bottom group, but
surely there will be considerable mixing in the large middle groups if not in the top group. Morever, with an integrated staff and with frank discussions of the problem I
should think a workable solution might be arrived at in
good faith. I would mix together all pupils, regardless of
ability, in a twelfth-grade course in problems of American
democracy.

In my first report I also recommended individualized
programs. I was specifically referring to the elective program. There would be no classification of students according to clearly defined and labeled tracks such as "college
preparatory," "vocational," "commercial," or "general."
In advising a student as to his elective program, the counselor is guided by the minimum program recommended as
a matter of school policy for the academically talented or
by recommended sequences leading to the development of
marketable skills. With such a system, many students of
similar abilities and interest have almost identical programs,
but there is no sharp line between different kinds of pro-

grams. Each year it is expected that the counselor will work with the student in appraising his record and planning his future elective courses. There is no fixed pattern of courses that, once enrolled in, a student must continue until graduation. Such individualized programs are perfectly compatible with ability grouping in required courses. A student with a vocational elective program may well sit in an English class with a future doctor. Something approaching automatic ability grouping takes place in the elective program; in physics, for example, one is likely to find only bright students.

The method of organizing a student's schedule I have just described may be contrasted with a form of programming that is called tracking. In this system, a student enrolls in or is assigned to a fixed program and stays with it until graduation. There is little or no individual counseling once the student decides which track he will follow. While still in grade 9, he will know exactly what courses he will take in each subsequent year. In some schools the student has little or no choice in determining his high school program. He is assigned to a particular track with its outline of courses he must study. His choice of electives is very small; he may, in fact, have no choice at all. His ability and past achievement determine the track in which he will be placed. At this point, tracking and ability grouping become synonymous, since all the pupils of given abilities will be found in the same track. Sometimes different diplomas are given.

I found few schools with strong track systems during my first study. However, Washington, D.C., in 1956 and St. Louis in 1958 embarked on a track program. As I see it, there are at least three reasons for such a system in these cities. First, with a great number of pupils and an overburdened counseling staff, the chances of individual attention from counselors are slim. Second, there is the problem of challenging slum children of high ability but low aspiration. Putting them in the top track does just this.

Third, there is also the problem of Latin for the slum children who cannot read English; eliminating Latin from the bottom track removes the temptation that parents will insist on their children studying this subject. Opponents of tracks say that they represent a poor substitute for guidance, that they are inflexible, and that they promote a caste system within the school as status is determined by which label a student carries with him—academic, vocational, general.

I am frank to say I am not prepared to take a stand on tracking in the large cities. Professional educators are themselves split on this issue. One must remember that the recommendation in my first report for individualized programs was meant for comprehensive high schools in certain kinds of communities—namely, communities in which not more than 50 per cent of the students went on to college, in which the median I.Q. of the student body was at the national average, and in which there was sufficient industry to provide jobs for pupils interested in developing marketable skills. My recommendations were written specifically for that type of community and not for the suburbs or the large cities.

The large cities are another story, and some kind of track scheme may indeed have merit. With limited guidance personnel and with pupils and parents indifferent if not hostile to education, assignment of pupils to tracks and restriction of electives may have much in its favor; the system of rigid tracks may be the only workable solution to a mammoth guidance problem.

## Personnel Problems

The shortage of guidance personnel leads me to a brief discussion of personnel problems in the large cities. Schools in wealthy suburban communities spend annually up to $1000 per pupil, an amount at least double that spent in the large cities. This vast difference in expenditure is due in large measure to differences in staffing policies, inasmuch as roughly 70 per cent of the budget (excluding capital outlay) goes to salaries. More specifically, the budgetary allotment for salaries is dependent upon two factors: the salaries paid to teachers and the number of teachers and other personnel employed. In wealthy suburban school districts teachers' salaries are higher than in the large cities, but the significant difference is in the number of personnel employed. A few wealthy school districts have as many as 70 professionals for 1000 students. (Professionals include not only teachers, but principals, librarians, guidance officers, the superintendent—in short, all personnel required to hold a certificate from the state.) In the suburban communities surrounding New York City the average is 60 professionals for 1000 pupils. These figures contrast sharply with the national average of about 40 professionals for 1000 pupils, which, in fact, is high in comparison with many large cities. Shortages are more severe in elementary than in secondary schools. The Educational Policies Commission of the National Education Association has called for 50 professionals for 1000 pupils, and I support this minimum figure as a realistic one to shoot at.

In any case, the discrepancy between forty and seventy staff members for the same number of pupils is dramatic, and, to my mind, highly disturbing. Such a discrepancy has many implications for our often stated goal of equality of opportunity. In view of the problems of the large cities and their importance to the national interest, I am of the opinion that these ratios might well be reversed, that the slum schools need considerably more staff than schools in well-to-do neighborhoods. This fact is recognized in Chicago and New York. In New York City, where the average is 40 professionals for 1000 pupils, there are "special service" schools in the slums which do, in fact, have additional personnel. These schools are defined by a formula that takes into account such factors as academic achievement, number of nonwhite and non-English-speaking children, student turnover rate, percentage of students provided free lunches, and so on. Even so, my guess is that these schools still fall considerably short of the staff that could be effectively utilized.

Within the large cities the problem is complicated by the fact that the turnover rate of teachers in the slum schools is very high. Teachers who have achieved some seniority rights often apply for transfer to schools away from the slum neighborhoods, where working conditions are at best difficult. The result is that slum schools are often staffed by either newly hired or substitute and emergency teachers. This is a real problem if one wishes to improve education in these neighborhoods. I suggest that school boards might examine the possibility of paying teachers in these schools more than teachers in other schools. One is bound to hear the argument that the problems of the teachers in slum areas differ in kind but not degree from the problems of the teachers in a wealthy neighborhood. I would reply by pointing out that the transfer requests speak for themselves. What I am suggesting does not sound so radical when one remembers the contrast in pay and staffing that is found between wealthy suburban districts and their poor neighbors. In any event, I think the seriousness of the problem in the slum schools necessitates at least a consideration of the ways in which top-flight teachers can be persuaded to remain in these difficult positions.

Allied to this general problem is the need in many cases to retrain teachers who, used to one type of pupil from middle-class families, suddenly find themselves engulfed with slum-area children whose values run directly counter to those of the teachers. Unless such teachers readjust their thinking, an impossible situation is at hand. Programs of in-service training for the teachers are a necessity if the schools are to serve a positive function in the community.

All the large cities have elaborate procedures for hiring

teachers and distributing them to schools. Often the cities set their own certification standards, which, in many cases, exceed those mandated by the state. To prevent patronage, a chronic problem in many districts in the nation, rigorous examination procedures with autonomous examining boards are established. It is unfortunate that these useful standards and examinations under present circumstances actually hinder what I consider desirable in the large cities—namely, a fully integrated staff. I have it on reliable authority that in one of the large cities with a very heavy Negro enrollment the school authorities would like to increase the number of Negro staff members but cannot do so because of the large number of failures on examinations. Upgrading the education of Negroes is the answer, of course, not relaxing the recruitment standards.

## Decentralization of Administration

In this chapter on school organization, I have tried to point up the necessity to match neighborhood needs and school services. Decisions made in the central office are remote from the many diverse neighborhoods that constitute the city and may or may not make sense in a particular school. In any event, this procedure tends to isolate the community from what goes on in the school. Some of the cities have recognized this problem to a greater or less extent. In New York City from 1949 to 1952, an experiment called the Bronx Park Project was conducted by the Board of Education, the Public Education Association, and Teachers College, Columbia University, with the aim of tying together the schools and the neighborhood. Unfortunately, this experiment has never been followed up and New York has remained in essence a highly centralized system.

In addition to a close alliance between the neighborhood and the school, there ought to be a single chain of authority running vertically from kindergarten through grade 12. Some school systems tend to be administered horizontally from a powerful central office with separate divisions for elementary, junior high, and senior high schools. New York is such a school system. One of the greatest weaknesses that I have found in my visits to schools across the nation is the lack of coordination, or articulation, between what is taught in the elementary, junior high, and senior high schools. Therefore I have urged that there be subject-matter coordination or supervision in grades K through 12 in *each* of the subject areas—not just art, music, or physical education, as is fairly common. This means a vertical chain of responsibility and authority.

To gain closer contact between school and community and to facilitate articulation of the educational program, Chicago has in the past few years taken steps to decentralize its system. The city has been divided into twenty separate districts, averaging about 27,000 students apiece. In each district there is a local superintendent responsible for the entire educational operation of grades K through 12. An attempt is made to give these local superintendents as much freedom and authority as is consonant with efficiency. It seems to me that this is a move forward. In effect, the school system of Chicago is composed of twenty separate school districts serving neighborhoods that are very diverse. Detroit and Philadelphia also have decentralized their administration; there are nine districts in Detroit and eight in Philadelphia, all with a district superintendent in charge of the schools from grades K through 12.

The problem is to achieve decentralization of line authority and responsibility without sacrificing the staff services that the central office can provide. These services are indeed extensive in the large cities. For example, in Chicago there is a long list of consultant services, each one of which has its own department and specialist personnel: curriculum development, libraries, research, visual education, health services, radio and television, to name but a few. Because of the large numbers of children involved, the big cities are able to provide at a minimum cost special facilities, personnel, and programs for what are called exceptional children. In St. Louis the central office coordinates a large staff of personnel for mentally retarded children, both completely deaf and hard-of-hearing children, partially seeing children, delinquent children, orthopedically handicapped and homebound children, and so on. City-wide testing programs are extremely valuable, as is the research which full-time personnel undertake. New York City has an extensive testing and research program.

## Grade Organization

Moving now to the grade structure of the large city school systems, I pointed out in my junior high report that there is no consistent pattern of organizational schemes in the United States. School systems vary tremendously in their structure. It is true that since the turn of the century more and more youth have begun their secondary education in grade 7 in either a separate junior high school or a combined junior-senior high school. The traditional 8-4 system has given way to the 6-3-3 and the 6-6; that is, six years of elementary school followed by six years of secondary school. In addition to these three basic patterns, there are many variations to be found throughout the nation, including 6-2-4, 5-3-4, and 7-5. The variety is due partly to the accidents of buildings available and other local conditions, but partly also to a lack of consensus among school people about where grade 9 belongs. Should ninth graders be included with senior high school pupils or should they be included with seventh and eighth graders? On the basis of professional disagreement and my own observations, I concluded in my junior high report that the grade structure of a school system was of less importance than the educational program provided. In turn, the educational program I believe satisfactory for seventh and eighth graders implies certain minimum enrollments for economical operation. This fact means that most eight-year elementary schools, which are very small neighborhood schools, cannot provide a suitable program for the seventh and eighth graders. Consequently a larger unit in the form of some kind of junior high school that will bring together more of these pupils from the elementary schools is the best answer for economical operation.

The exception to this reasoning is likely to occur in the very large cities, where high density of population means large enrollments in the neighborhood elementary schools. It may be possible, therefore, to provide a suitable educational program for seventh and eighth graders in an eight-year elementary school. In fact, however, the very large cities are organized generally on a 6-3-3 basis: New York, Los Angeles, Philadelphia, Baltimore, Houston, Cleveland, and Washington. Chicago has been organized on an 8-4 basis since the abolition of junior high schools for economy in 1932–33, but it is now moving in the direction of reorganizing grades 7 and 8 with the establishment of what are called "upper grade centers" for those grades. Each upper grade center, housed in an elementary school, draws students from several elementary schools. Chicago is, then, a reorganized 8-4 system in terms of housing. Junior high schools also existed in St. Louis but were discontinued in the thirties. Since then the city has been organized on an 8-4 basis. In order to provide for industrial arts and homemaking, special centers were set up many years ago throughout the city, and the seventh and eighth graders travel to these centers from their respective elementary schools. There apparently is widespread dissatisfaction with this scheme because of travel inconvenience and traffic dangers.

The situation in Detroit, like that in Chicago, is somewhat in flux. Like many other cities, Detroit adopted the

6-3-3 plan early in this century; however, as the city grew and annexed surrounding communities, it also incorporated their school systems, which were generally not organized on a 6-3-3 basis. The depression hindered the development of junior high schools. At present about 50 per cent of the seventh and eighth graders are in separate junior high schools. A new pattern has been developed recently—namely, the incorporation of grade 9 into the elementary schools to provide a junior high school unit, grades 7 through 9, within a number of elementary schools. Though this unit is handled separately from the elementary school, it is in the same building. In terms of housing, then, Detroit may be said to be moving toward a combined 9-3 and 6-3-3 system.

Both Detroit and Chicago provide illustration of the importance of putting program before organization. In each case attempts are being made to provide satisfactory instruction without the expense that would be involved in commencing an extensive building program of separate junior high schools. To change any organizational scheme is likely to entail considerable expense. Therefore critics of junior high schools in the large cities where the 6-3-3 pattern is firmly established must also face the problem of coming up with a satisfactory alternative that will not be prohibitively expensive. My conclusion still holds: The structure of the system is less important than the program provided.

## Specialized High Schools

A concern for both the quality of the program and economy of operation has led most of the large cities to establish specialized high schools. Most have specialized vocational high schools; a very few have selective academic high schools. To duplicate, in particular, the vocational courses in each high school throughout the city would be prohibitively expensive; and since the school enrollment is so large, separate high schools are feasible. Moreover, since there is such diversity in vocational opportunities within the city as a whole, it would be impossible to have vocational programs in each school that would reflect the over-all employment situation. For the same reason, a labor-management advisory committee that would function adequately could not be provided for each school. This situation is in direct contrast, of course, to that in a fairly small industrial city with only one high school that must of necessity be comprehensive in its offerings. These specialized schools generally enroll students from all over the city, whereas the general high school is a neighborhood school with a certain attendance area.

In New York City there are eighty-six high schools, and twenty-nine of them are vocational schools. In addition there are three selective academic high schools. Eleven schools require all applicants to take qualifying examinations for entrance: Stuyvesant High School, Bronx High School of Science, Brooklyn Technical High School (the three selective academic high schools), High School of Music and Art, School of Performing Arts, High School of Art and Design, High School of Fashion Industries, Aviation High School, New York School of Printing, Brooklyn High School of Automotive Trades, and Samuel Gompers Vocational High School. Many more of the vocational high schools require entrance examinations for certain fields of specialization.

There are at least two problems that arise with the operation of separate vocational schools in both the large cities and surrounding suburban areas. First, there is the very practical matter of location and transportation. I have noted that New York City has an excellent array of vocational programs in schools scattered throughout the city. Boys and girls with special interests have relatively little difficulty in attending the vocational school of their choice because of the ease of public transportation to all parts of that city. To point up the importance of accessibility, one notes that there are no separate vocational schools in Los Angeles, where there is practically no public transportation in the district, which is 54 miles from end to end. In suburban areas, where demand in local high schools for vocational education is slight, one sometimes finds vocational schools serving a number of communities. New Jersey has a system of county vocational schools, and one finds that youth with vocational interests in suburban Essex County, for example, attend the county vocational school. But it is much easier and perhaps more desirable from the students' point of view to attend the local high school with the friends they may have grown up with than to travel some distance to a vocational school.

The second problem involves a conflict of interest one sometimes finds between those responsible for vocational schools and those responsible for the general high schools. The conflict in large cities arises over the responsibility for the countless slow learners who are suited neither for vocational programs with high standards nor for academic work. The general high school people resent being left with these students, and the vocational people resent attempts to pass them along to vocational schools. I venture to suggest that both sides in the argument have responsibilities and, above all, that what is needed is a vertical organizational structure to ensure that what may be two warring factions get together to solve a very important and difficult problem.

With respect to specialized, selective high schools for academically talented youth, these schools have flourished in large Eastern cities—New York City, Boston, Philadelphia—but have never spread west of the Mississippi River. There is no question that these schools furnish a good academic education for those selected for admission.

Selective academic schools are practicable in a large

city principally because of large numbers of pupils in the city. The selective academic high schools in New York City by no means drain off all the academic talent from the general high schools. A respectable road to college stays open via the neighborhood high school, where there remain sufficient numbers of bright students to maintain a tone of serious learning. Were separate selective schools to be established in smaller communities, I should be concerned that either the school would enroll too few students to be economical or else would drain off too much of the academic talent from the neighborhood high school. In a suburban community I am sure that the parental pressures for admission of children without sufficient ability would be as severe as pressures for admission to a top track if a track system were instituted. It is well, too, to bear in mind an important difference between a school like the Bronx High School of Science and a European pre-university school—namely, the fact that the European schools in contrast to American selective schools fail a large percentage of their students each year and eliminate them from the school. I cannot envision this sort of thing happening in any American community! In my first report I discussed selective academic high schools briefly, and voiced a conclusion which, as far as I am concerned, still holds:

"I should not want to argue for the elimination of selective academic high schools in the cities in which these schools are now successful, but I would raise many questions about the establishment of such a school in another city of equal size and more serious questions still if such a school were to be suggested for a city served by only a few high schools. The historical traditions of the selective schools in the East are well-known factors in their success.

"Furthermore, if my conclusions . . . are correct, it is unnecessary to establish selective academic high schools for the education of the academically talented. . . . The improvement of the comprehensive high school would seem to offer far more promise for the improvement of American education than the introduction of selective academic high schools into communities where, hitherto, they have not existed."

I shall note in a later chapter the challenge that a school like the Bronx High School of Science provides for the comprehensive high schools with respect to the education of bright students. Moreover, though I am a strong supporter of comprehensive high schools on the grounds of the desirability of a situation in which the future corporation executive is in the same school with the future factory worker, I am under no illusion that such a school can always overcome the strong divisive community attitudes one sometimes finds.

Supporters of selective academic high schools can argue that selective schools, by drawing students from every section of the city, are more truly comprehensive with respect to the background of the students than are the neighborhood schools which serve particular communities within the city. The question comes back to the impracticality of integrating socio-economic groups to any great extent. As I earlier indicated, one cannot imagine the possibility of a wealthy suburban district deliberately consolidating with other districts to achieve a truly comprehensive high school in which students of all abilities and socio-economic backgrounds will study together. Although theoretically comprehensive, since they serve all the youth of the community, some suburban high schools more nearly resemble certain private schools than they do widely comprehensive high schools. Indeed I know of at least one private school that, because of its extensive scholarship policy, could be termed a kind of national public school, in that it draws students from all over the country and from different socio-economic backgrounds. One might make the argument that this school is more comprehensive than the public school in a wealthy suburb. In short, one must be very careful in arguing about advantages of one type of school or another without regard for the socio-economic composition of the high school population.

## The School Board

No discussion of the organization and structure of educational systems in large cities would be complete without at least a brief mention of the all-important school board. Honest and intelligent citizens devoted to the best interests of public education are a necessity for good schools. How to assure attainment of this goal is the problem.

In this regard the story of Chicago from 1933 to 1946 is interesting as an illustration of what can be done. In this period major changes in the administrative set-up took place. First, the Illinois legislature changed a law that had enabled Chicago to operate with a three-headed organizational structure; that is, three different administrators reported directly to the school board. The change in the law created a single executive officer responsible for the whole school system. At this point I must make plain my conviction that there ought to be one executive, and only one, directly responsible to the board of education, and he should be the superintendent of schools. At least one large city—St. Louis—violates what seems to me this basic principle of sound management. Such people as the business manager and building and grounds manager should answer to the superintendent.

In Chicago the manner of selection of school board members was also changed. The mayor continued to appoint board members, but he chose them from among nominees put forward by a large caucus committee composed of respected people from numerous civic, labor, and business groups throughout the city. As I understand it, this procedure has worked well ever since, with the full cooperation of the mayor. With the growing tradition of a top-flight school board and the effort through decentralized administration to bring the schools into closer touch with the various neighborhoods within the city, Chicago seems to be a kind of model pointing the way to sound educational structure in those big cities where politics and education are still clearly enmeshed.

At the end of August, 1961, the New York State legislature provided for the appointment of a new school board for New York City. This action was the result of charges of waste and corruption in the administration of the city's school system. The selection of board members in the future is to follow the Chicago pattern. The mayor will make appointments to the board from a list of nominees put forward by a panel of civic leaders. This mechanism is clearly a major step forward and is in line with the recommendation made by a committee headed by President Heald of the Ford Foundation in 1959. The change was long overdue. Charges of waste and corruption in administration naturally lead to suspicion of the quality of teaching in the schools. I have indicated that members of my staff saw some excellent teaching in brief visits to New York City junior high schools. But if public confidence is to be restored, the facts, whatever they may be, ought to be known through a full-scale investigation of the quality of instruction. As the largest American city, New York ought to be in the forefront of sound public education.

# CHAPTER IV
## The College-Oriented Suburbs

To drive a car or to ride a train through a wealthy suburb and then through a city slum is for many people an everyday experience. As seen from the car or train window, the basic contrast is one of housing, the congested city blocks contrasting with the more spacious and attractive suburban homes. Although sensitive Americans might find the comparison painful, it is as nothing when compared with the profoundly shocking experience of going from a high school that serves a wealthy suburb to one that serves a slum. The last three chapters have been largely devoted to making the reader visualize the social conditions in the slums of large cities as reflected in the schools. As a vivid contrast, let me now turn to the problems in the suburban high school, with which far more readers will be familiar as a result of their own experience.

I shall not stress the contrast in the buildings or the physical facilities, though they are startling enough. For, to be quite frank, I am not at all convinced that in terms of education the dazzling attractiveness of the spacious buildings of some suburban schools I know are as much of an asset as they seem, though I hasten to add that many large city schools should be torn down and replaced by modern structures. The real contrast is evident only to a visitor who will take the time to visit classes, talk to the principals and teachers in both schools, examine the relevant statistics, and ascertain the completely different educational aspirations of the families.

The problems besetting the teachers and guidance

officers in the school in the low-income area in the big city
I have discussed at length in the previous chapters. These
problems to a large extent reflect the cultural level and
parental ambitions of the homes from which the children
come. So, too, do the tasks facing the staff of a high school
in a wealthy suburb. But they are almost the reverse of
those presented to the teachers in many large city schools.
The overriding consideration in the type of community I
wish to consider is the parental demand that their offspring
obtain admittance to a four-year college. Indeed, a convenient index of the social composition of a school district
is the percentage of high school graduates who go on with
full-time education. The percentage is remarkably constant
year by year if a community is not undergoing marked
expansion, contraction, or social change. Nationwide, some
50 per cent of high school graduates go on for some kind
of further education. In the suburbs the figure may run
from 50 per cent to over 90 per cent.

The heavily college-oriented suburb is the subject of
this chapter. When one finds a high school from which 80
per cent or more of the graduates regularly enroll in some
four-year college or university, one can be certain that a
relatively homogeneous residential community is at hand.
In such a suburb the vast majority of the inhabitants belong
to the managerial or professional class; the average level of
income is high; the real estate values are correspondingly
elevated. In these wealthy communities, one is likely to
find effective school boards, great parental interest in the
public schools, high expenditure per pupil. Since the citizens are interested in good schools and ample resources are
available, the public schools are as good as the professionals
know how to make them.

One could name a dozen or two communities in the
large metropolitan areas of New York, Philadelphia, and
Chicago where schools of this sort exist. These schools have
become nationally famous for their excellence and are

sometimes referred to as "lighthouse" schools, beacons light-
ing the way toward educational progress. There can be no
doubt of the excellence of the teaching in the schools in
the lighthouse school districts. Large school budgets enable
the superintendent and the principals of the schools to re-
cruit a corps of first-rate teachers; the level of the salaries
is far higher than in many other districts. Furthermore the
size of the staff in proportion to the size of the student body
is as much as 75 per cent greater than in the corresponding
schools in the nearby large central city. Physical facilities
are usually the envy of those who live in less-prosperous
school districts. In short, the high costs per pupil are an
essential factor in assuring the excellence of these schools.

Yet it would be a mistake to assume that the high expenditures are the only factor. In addition to a top-flight
teaching staff, the lighthouse schools are fortunate in the
nature of the student body. The vast majority of pupils
come from homes that are by no means typical in the
United States. The attitude of the parents toward education,
toward music, art, drama, literature, and politics is far
different from that of the average American family. Most
of the fathers and many of the mothers are college graduates. Shall we say the cultural level and degree of social
sophistication are extremely high? Taking the community
as a whole and comparing it with most other school districts
of comparable size, I think some such description to be
warranted.

Many of these well-to-do families who some years ago
would have sent their children to private schools now find
the costs prohibitive and admission difficult because of increasing selectivity at the better-known private schools.
Consequently they look to the public schools to provide the
same degree of academic excellence and the same assurance
of college admission that the top prep schools traditionally
have provided. The result is that the public high schools
in these heavily college-oriented communities have reverted

to the sole function that most high schools had at the turn of the century; namely, that of preparing youth for college. As I travel about the country, I sense that the public schools in many suburban communities have accepted this challenge. What it amounts to is a stronger academic emphasis than has been present in American public education in some time. To my mind, it is still insufficient in many otherwise excellent schools, particularly with regard to the breadth of the education open to the bright students. In the next chapter I shall attempt to document this statement and assess the blame.

Suburban schools today are challenged to "get" boys and girls into top-flight colleges and consequently to maintain high standards in the academic courses. These schools are also faced with a dilemma. The problem comes in cases where the parental ambitions outrun the offspring's ability; that is, where the boy or girl has difficulty mastering academic work in a school with high standards and yet is expected by his parents to attend a prestige college. If the student with limited ability fails to gain admission to a prestige college, the parents are likely to blame the public school, little realizing that the same student in a private school would probably fare no better. The situation has changed since the time when by dint of hard work and extra tutoring even a dull boy could be admitted to Harvard, Yale, or Princeton. Not that such a boy today is prohibited from admission to college. Far from it. There are colleges today for every kind of student with every degree of ability.

Since one of the larger worries of suburban parents is closely identified with higher education in general, no discussion of education in the suburbs can avoid bringing in the whole variety of patterns and purposes of American higher education. Therefore in the next few pages I shall try to help clarify the confusing subject of the development of the American college and university and to tie in my thoughts about the relationship of schools, colleges, and professional training. I think this discussion bears directly upon the concern of parents in the college-oriented suburbs.

## The Pattern of American College Education

The American four-year liberal arts college is almost an historical accident. The colleges of the colonial days acquired the right to award the first degree in arts (the bachelor's degree), and they and their successors have clung desperately to this right. Four years became the standard amount of time to be spent by a student in a college for the purpose of obtaining this first degree. Until the second half of the nineteenth century the subjects on which the college student was examined were essentially rhetoric, mathematics, Greek and Latin, and the history and literature of antiquity. In this period the study of law and medicine was on the same footing as the study for the first degree. High school graduates entered directly into the best law and medical schools in the United States. Postgraduate instruction and higher degrees were essentially unknown.

About the middle of the last century, the impact of science and invention on the industrialized nations began to have reverberations in educational circles. In Germany, France, and Great Britain proposals were put forward to establish new institutions to train men who would construct, operate, and understand machines. In the United States the reform educational movement took a rather special turn because of the predominantly agricultural nature of the economy. Agricultural and mechanical arts colleges were established and gained both respectability and support by the passage of the Morrill Act by Congress in 1862. Thus started a process which has continued right down to the present day—a process of expanding the variety of subjects regarded as suitable for college work.

The stimulus to public education by the passage of the

Morrill Act was, of course, only one factor making for expansion of educational facilities in those states where private colleges had not yet taken root. The demand for practical education as apart from classical education had been manifest before the Civil War in the older states. For example, a report of a committee of the Massachusetts legislature in 1850 was critical of Harvard College and declared that "a college should be open to boys who seek specific learning for a specific purpose. It should give the people the practical instruction they want and not a classical literary course suitable only for an aristocracy. It should help young men to become better farmers, mechanics, and merchants." The Harvard authorities then and later disagreed as to the applicability of this doctrine to their institution. So, too, did the trustees of all the older eastern colleges. Nevertheless, after the Civil War even these colleges began to broaden their ideas about what constituted a college education.

Charles W. Eliot, who became President of Harvard in 1869, led the movement to introduce the elective system. The definition of "arts and sciences" was expanded to include modern foreign languages, history, political science, economics, and the physical and biological sciences. In this century the process continued; the spectral band of curricular offerings was widened by the inclusion of sociology and the separation of psychology from philosophy. At this point, however, the widening of the band ceased in the older four-year colleges. In these conservative institutions the faculties resisted the inclusion of more practical courses in the programs leading to the A.B. or B.S. degrees and have continued to hold the line to the present day.

## Professional Education and National Welfare

Universities, both private and public, commonly are composed of many faculties, each with jurisdiction over a degree program. During the last quarter of the nineteenth century and the first two quarters of the twentieth century, there has been continual discussion of whether the professional faculties should or should not award a *first* degree for a professional program. Engineering and agriculture early became fields in which a four-year course of study became recognized as adequate for professional preparation, and successful candidates received the B.S. degree. Education was later given the same status, and about the same time (i.e., the turn of the century) the old normal schools became teachers colleges and started to grant a bachelor's degree to their graduates. In the last fifty years, the number of undergraduate professional or semiprofessional programs has inceased greatly. For example, journalism, social work, nursing, pharmacy, forestry, home economics, business and commerce have all become accepted subjects for undergraduate study in at least some universities. Even some of the liberal arts colleges have widened the spectral band of their academic offerings by including a variety of practical courses, though none perhaps can boast of as wide a spectrum of formal education as can a state university or a private university in a very large city.

The consequences of the development I have briefly sketched are well known. There are over one thousand institutions which offer programs of study leading to a bachelor of arts degree, and there is a bewildering assortment of subjects included in the bill of fare. Over sixteen hundred different kinds of academic degrees are currently awarded in the United States.

At the same time that the undergraduate programs were expanding, two ancient professions, law and medicine, developed their training schools in a direction one may call European. The better law and medical schools became postgraduate schools. Today they require for admission either a first degree or at least three years of undergraduate study. A few schools of education and business administration have followed suit, and the graduate schools of arts and sciences have expanded enormously in the last fifty years. Therefore, at present we have in most universities two levels of professional and semiprofessional training— one at the undergraduate level, the other at the graduate level.

As a rough approximation, it can be said that something like 5 to 8 per cent (see Table 1) of a given age group

TABLE 1: *Selected Professional Degrees Awarded 1958–1959*

|  | Men | Women | Total |
|---|---|---|---|
| Law | 9,661 | 264 | 9,925 |
| Medicine (including dentistry) | 9,630 | 388 | 10,018 |
| Theology | 4,989 | ...... | 4,989 |
| Engineering | 38,013 | 121 | 38,134 |
| Master's degrees* | 47,321 | 22,176 | 69,497 |
| Doctorates† | 8,371 | 989 | 9,360 |
| Total | 117,985 | 23,938 | 141,923 |
| Registered births in 1935 | 1,105,489 | 1,049,616 | 2,155,105 |
| Professional degrees in 1958–59 as a percentage of births in 1935 (average age of degree recipient assumed to be 24) | 10.7% | 2.3% | 6.6% |

\* Includes degrees beyond the bachelor's or first professional level but below the doctorate. This category does *not* include such degrees as Master of Library Science, Master of Social Work, Master of Business Administration, etc., when these constitute first professional degrees.

† All professions included.

(This table was derived from *Earned Degrees Conferred 1958–1959*, U.S. Office of Education Circular No. 636, U.S. Government Printing Office, Washington, 1961.)

receive professional degrees each year in the United States. A similar percentage in Great Britain and the free European nations are enrolled in universities. One may call these students the future members of the learned professions. As to the significance of this group for the welfare of the nation, no argument is required. Our future may well depend on how successful we are in identifying and educating to the full those students who have the ability later to attain professional university degrees, including the doctor's degree in science, social science, and the humanities. The vigorous reappraisal of public high schools which has been going on all over the nation since the Russian success with rockets indicates our awareness of this need. To my mind, the present 5 to 8 per cent of an age group in university work should be doubled, though not in every field. For example, we are short of doctors but not of lawyers.

## Academic Talent

In this matter of developing talent through education, there is no antithesis between national welfare and concern for the individual. Whichever interest one has, the conclusion is the same. All who can benefit from the training should be enrolled in professional schools of the universities. Thus it may well be argued that the insistence of suburban parents on having their children prepared for entrance into colleges, and even into specific colleges where particularly high standards are known to prevail, is not only in the best interest of the child but in the best interest of the nation as well.

Yet anyone who has had experience in teaching in a secondary school or college knows that the mere desire on the part of a youth or parent is not enough to ensure a career as a professional man or woman. To be sure, keen desire must be present, willingness to work hard on academic subjects must be a characteristic of the future doctor or lawyer, and, as maturity increases, there must also develop something approaching a passion for the subject. But over and above these traits of character, the aspirant for a professional degree must have certain aptitudes for academic work. How can these be determined? By noting the judgment of the teachers, particularly in English and in arithmetic in the lower grades, and by considering the scores on a series of scholastic aptitude or intelligence tests. I have examined the programs of many thousands of high school students in various parts of the United States and noted the scores on tests of those who were successfully carrying a heavy academic program. On the basis of such evidence, I suggest that if a student in grade 9 has a consistent score on a scholastic aptitude or intelligence test which places him in the upper 15 or 20 per cent of the high school population *on a national basis,* then the presumption is that he is academically talented. In my judgment, this student ought to think in terms of a professional career and ought to elect a heavy academic program beyond the minimum required of all students.

In the average high school where not more than 50 per cent of the students go on to college, and where the average scholastic aptitude expressed in I.Q. terms is not much above 100, the number of academically talented students will be roughly 15 to 20 per cent of the student body. In contrast, in wealthy suburban schools where 80 per cent or more go on to college, the average I.Q. score is likely to be 115 or higher. In this case, half the students have scores as high as the top 15 to 20 per cent nationally. In such a school, I suggest that the presumption ought to be, therefore, that about half the students have academic talents clustered in such a way that they can study effectively and rewardingly in grades 9 through 12 the following minimum program of eighteen academic subjects in addition to physical education and other nonacademic electives like art, music, and typing: four years of English, three years of social studies, four years of mathematics, four years of one foreign language, and three years of science. Those who stand out in arithmetic in grade 7 should be urged to start algebra in grade 8. In addition, most if not all students will begin a foreign language on a conversational basis in grade 7. Whether the assumption that a student is academically talented is sound can be discovered only by trial and error. My definition is really operational. If the student elects the recommended program and in spite of all the good will in the world finds that it is too heavy, then clearly the diagnosis was incorrect and the guidance officer ought to urge him to drop one or more of the courses. If the marks in all five courses in grade 9 are at least satisfactory, the student should be urged to continue the same course of study the following year. The guidance officer thus follows the student's progress closely throughout high school. Students electing such a program of academic studies will, of course, proceed to college, university, or engineering school. They will be, in my opinion, well prepared for the next stage in their academic voyage toward the goal of becoming professional men and women.

Why do I say "well prepared"? To answer this question, of course, is to answer the question as to why my recommended high school program is the right one for the academically talented student. Specifically it is to say why in addition to four years of English and at least three years of social studies so much mathematics, science, and foreign language are included. In a few words, the reason is that when these talented youth go on to college they should be so prepared that all doors will be open to them. That is to say, when they leave high school they should be equipped with the kinds of skills and competencies which will enable them in college to choose any one of a number of roads leading to a profession. Take mathematics, physics and chemistry, for example. Unless a college freshman has studied four hard years of high school mathematics and the eleventh and twelfth grade science courses, it will be extremely difficult for him to major in a physical or biological science. With only ninth and tenth grade mathematics, a future career as a doctor or a research scientist is almost closed to a college student. Even in the social sciences,

mathematics is becoming increasingly important, and freshman college mathematics courses are difficult if not impossible for those who enter with only a year or two of high
school mathematics. In my first report I have discussed the
case for foreign languages at some length and will not
repeat my observations on that subject except to say that
career opportunities are opening rapidly for persons skilled
in a foreign language. Finally, once in college, a student
who has had a wide academic background in high school
is free to spend his time on courses at a level corresponding
to his maturity and on courses not offered in high school.

In short, my recommended program for academically
talented students is designed to keep doors open, to prevent
early specialization by students with many talents. It is
true that these students should go on to college and then on
to graduate school and professional careers, but I wish to
stress that this is not *the* college preparatory program. As I
hope I made clear, we have in the United States a wide
variety of colleges and admission requirements; there is no
single college preparatory program, and the sooner that
phrase is dropped the better. Secondly, the program I
recommended is tough—students will say so—but this fact
has nothing to do with the value of a wide academic program. Latin and Greek are tough, but I have not recommended them. Finally, I make no assumptions about the
value of such a program in training or disciplining the mind.
I believe talented students should develop specific skills in
high school that, if not developed, restrict their choice of
careers. I do not have to emphasize that this statement
holds for students in both suburban and slum schools.

## The Significance of the Advanced
## Placement Program

Today the future student in a professional school may
spend as little as three years in an undergraduate college.

For a few highly gifted students it is possible to obtain
a bachelor's degree in this period of time, thanks to a
significant movement which has rapidly gained momentum
in the last ten years. I refer to the Advanced Placement
Program. The colleges and schools involved in this endeavor
permit the most able students to take freshman college
courses in the last year of high school. The success or
failure in these courses is determined by subject-matter
examinations set by the colleges themselves and administered by the Educational Testing Service. The college
decides whether those who pass the examinations are placed
in more advanced sections of a given subject—the sophomore level of mathematics, for example—and whether
credit is given toward the bachelor's degree. For the very
able students, as much as one year's credit may be earned
and the college course thus shortened to three years. Since
I am an enthusiastic supporter of Advanced Placement, I
am glad to report that in 1960-1961 something like 13,000
students took 17,000 exams and well over 600 colleges were
involved. The top ten colleges in terms of numbers of
candidates included six of the Ivy League institutions,
Massachusetts Institute of Technology, University of Mich-
igan, Stanford, and Northwestern. In one institution,
Harvard, about half of the entering class in 1961 partici-
pated in the program and nearly ten per cent passed enough
examinations to be eligible for sophomore standing.

The advantages of gaining a year for those who are going on to study law or medicine or enroll in a graduate school
of arts and sciences hardly need be emphasized. The success
of the Advanced Placement Program in the last few years
is one of the most encouraging signs of real improvement
in our educational system. Needless to say, only a high
school of considerable size and adequate financial resources
could possibly offer college freshman courses to twelfth
graders in the eleven different subjects in which the
examinations are given. Therefore, how widely such a

scheme can spread will depend to a large degree on w
in many states, the consolidation of small high school
proceed. To my mind, every high school ought to str
to provide the opportunity for advanced placement in at
least one subject, no matter how few candidates there may
be. Interested citizens may wish to inquire whether their
own high school is one of those participating in the Advanced Placement Program.

## Standards for College Admission

From time to time it has been suggested that to ensure the
best possible use of the student's time during the college
years, the colleges themselves ought to raise their admission standards. Even those that are now highly selective
could be more demanding, it is thought. In this way the
colleges could make certain that their students would have
completed the elementary phases of all the basic academic
subjects in high school and could use their college years to
the best advantage.

The problems that confront one are enormous if one
contemplates raising standards for admission to undergraduate programs in all kinds of colleges. The number
of institutions involved is well over fifteen hundred. What
is far more significant, the variety of programs offered is
such that no one can make a reasonable argument for any
uniform requirements for admission to *all* the programs
except the ability to read and write the English language,
and even this requirement is often honored in the breach.
In addition, standards for the first degree are almost as
diverse as the standards for admission. The officers in
charge of admission to graduate schools of law, medicine,
business, and arts and sciences are well aware of this fact.
They know what many Americans also know; namely, that
the mere holding of a bachelor's degree has almost no
significance. Yet no one would publish a rank list of institu-

hether,
can
ve

illing to be quoted publicly to the effect
ecord in one college has about the same
cord in another. In the United States
of institutions granting the first degree
cy of silence as to the existence of such
consequence of the American doctrine
, and I do not decry it. It does render
any serious contemplation of raising
university entrance requirements the country
over in order to improve the work of the high schools.

## A Radical New Proposal

A great deal of the criticism of our high schools one hears
today comes from members of the professions, particularly
the doctors and lawyers. I suggest that the key to raising
standards lies in the hands of just those critics. Unless
members of the learned professions are willing to say what
degree of minimum mastery of academic disciplines their
future colleagues should attain, how can they justly com-
plain about the lack of standards in American education?

The present admission policies of the graduate schools
may be in general adequate—that is, adequate in terms of
the purely professional aspects of their work. Yet I venture
to make a plea for a radical reform. Specifically, *what I
urge is that the leading professional schools of law and
medicine and graduate schools of arts and sciences require
their candidates to pass a set of examinations which would
demonstrate a mastery of academic subjects somewhat comparable to that required for entrance into a European
university*. The requirements might be as follows: the
ability to write a competent essay; a good reading, writing,
and speaking knowledge of at least one modern foreign
language; a knowledge of mathematics through the calculus;
knowledge of physics, chemistry, and biology at the freshman level of our most rigorous colleges; at the same level

of competence, knowledge of American history and political institutions and English and American literature. If such standards were to be imposed, of course, due notice must be given. A five-year waiting period would allow the effect of such a revolutionary announcement to affect not only college work but high school work as well. Let me point out that the level of accomplishment I am suggesting is less than that attained by the European who enters a university with something approaching a mastery of at least two languages (not necessarily two modern languages, of course).

Those who enter the professional schools must be among the academically talented; otherwise they would never have succeeded in making the records in school and college which have earned them admission to the highly selective first-rate graduate schools. Since they are academically talented, it seems clear to me from what I have observed in high school that all of them might have been well advanced in mathematics, science, history, literature, and a foreign language by the time they entered college. If the majority of those students in the future were to complete such a program of high school studies, the college would have little to do to help them meet the new requirements for admission to the graduate school. An option among the present variety of college programs would still remain. Only those who had failed to take advantage of the opportunities in school (or came from poor schools) would have to use some of their time in college studying elementary mathematics, science, and a foreign language.

Only at the interface between college and professional graduate school is it conceivable that national standards of *achievement* in subject-matter areas could be proclaimed and enforced. The number of institutions involved would be relatively small, perhaps several hundred at the most, and the number of applicants each year not more than 10 to 15 per cent of an age group. Thus the problems that, at

the college-entrance level, seem to me virtually insurmountable, are at the graduate level by no means over-
whelmingly difficult. I might note that commencing in the
fall of 1961 candidates for admission to law schools will be
required to take two new tests that will supplement the
currently used aptitude examination. One is a test of writing skills and the other a test of general background in the
areas of science, humanities, and the social sciences.

## The Suburban Dilemma

It is clear that the way our collegiate pattern has developed
one group of colleges is open only to the highly gifted
(top 3 per cent) or the academically talented. The highly
gifted may be able to finish the college course even in the
highly selective colleges in three years. The academically
talented youth has a chance of admission. Of course, no one
institution is likely to be in a position to admit all the
academically talented who apply—not even all the highly
gifted may be accepted. But unless the academic talent of a
high school senior places him in the top 15 or 20 per cent
on a national basis, his chance of gaining admission to some
of the well-known colleges is slight indeed. Even in schools
in the most heavily college-oriented communities, the
academically talented students constitute not more than
half the student body. To carry the program I outlined
earlier is for many students far too heavy an academic burden. That is to say, it is too much if high standards in the
courses are maintained and the boy or girl in question is to
benefit from the course of study. What of those who are not
among the academically talented but whose parents insist
upon their attending a prestige college?

If one could measure the degree of collective parental
worry about college admission, I feel quite confident that
the intensity of the worry would be proportional to the
number of Ivy League graduates resident in the community

in question. Because of the rapid rise in the number of applicants in the past few years, these so-called prestige colleges are increasingly selective and are becoming pre-university institutions; that is, institutions from which many students, most of whom are exceptionally bright, go on for graduate study of some sort. To my mind, the fact that considerably more than half of those who receive the bachelor's degree from institutions like Harvard, Yale, and Princeton now go on to study in a professional or graduate school is of great significance and should be widely publicized.

I have known fathers who were aggrieved because their sons were not admitted to a particular prestige college and yet who admitted readily that the boy in question was not fitted for study in a graduate or professional school in the same university. It is much easier for such fathers to understand that their sons are unlikely candidates as lawyers or doctors than it is for them to understand that their sons do not have the ability to get through Harvard, Princeton, or Yale. Once it is widely known that these institutions enroll predominantly future professional people with considerable academic talent, I suspect pressures from suburban parents will ease. High school students themselves without professional ambition will think twice about applying to an institution in which the large bulk of students will continue their education beyond the A.B. degree. I am assuming then that in the public mind certain institutions will be associated with high-level academic interests and that social considerations, the fact that the "right" people go there, will be less of a factor motivating parents and students in the wealthy suburbs.

At the same time students may attach more importance to learning as a step toward a professional career rather than as a means to college admission. Allied to this point is the fact that some suburban school people are concerned that their graduates, after admission to top-notch institutions, fail to come up to expectations. This problem of the gentleman's "C" has, of course, plagued some of the private schools for many years. Increasing competition in the prestige colleges for places in graduate schools may alleviate the problem somewhat by providing still another major hurdle for the student. That the realities of the situation with respect to the nature of the student body in Ivy League colleges is becoming more widely known may be inferred from the fact that applications dropped off 6 per cent last year.

Those whose school marks and college board test scores place them outside the group of the academically talented should seek admission to other types of colleges or universities. This is the lesson that suburban parents must learn. In fact, the guidance officer or counselor in the high school will have discussed the matter with the youth and with the family over a course of years and will have emphasized just the points I have been making. Indeed he may go further and say to a distressed father, "Conditions have changed since you graduated in the 1930s when the college you mention so often was admitting almost all who applied. The caliber of the student body in that same college is now so superior in terms of academic talent and the academic pace so brisk that your son would be bound to fail out if by some accident he were admitted. The admission officer would be doing you both a disservice if an exception were made in your son's case and he were admitted." If the father then demands to know what can be done to meet his and the boy's ambition to earn a bachelor's degree, a resourceful, experienced counselor in a college-oriented school will produce a list of colleges whose admission policies and programs are better adapted to the limited academic talents of the son. *I have been assured by just such counselors that there exists such a wide range of private and public institutions that almost any boy who reaches the senior high school class in a suburban school can obtain admission to some four-year college.* Whether he is well advised to do so is another matter. I am sure that a two-year junior college or technical institute would be better suited for some who now hunt desperately for entry into four-year institutions.

The pattern of higher education varies so much state by state that one cannot generalize about it. In wealthy eastern suburbs, the institutions that parents consider are usually private colleges and universities. However, the best illustration of the operation of the junior college is found in the large public system of higher education in California. There the junior college system is a legal extension of secondary education. There were sixty-three such colleges in California in 1959 (more than in any other state), each being under the control of a board elected by the district served. The finances are provided by local taxes and state aid. The curricula in these junior colleges are widely comprehensive. The students, almost all of whom live at home, may be pursuing their studies either with the intent of transferring to one of the seven campuses of the University of California after two years, or with the notion of obtaining employment at the end of their course of study. The ratio of transfer students to terminal students varies from place to place and year to year. For 1956 in the state as a whole, some 67 per cent of the students were in the transfer category. By no means all who have the intent to transfer succeed, however, in meeting the standard set by the University of California for admission to the junior year. Certain courses must be passed with certain grades, and every effort is made to have the standards in the junior colleges comparable with those in force in the freshman and sophomore courses in the university itself. A majority of the students are enrolled on a full-time basis, but a considerable number attend part time. In addition to performing the functions I have described, the California community colleges provide many courses for adults and serve in this way as important educational centers.

I am frank to confess that the pattern of higher education in California seems to me a highly promising one for the United States in the second half of the twentieth century. Opportunity is provided locally for education beyond the high school. For those who have the ability and the interest, the first two years of academic college work can be accomplished with a minimum of expense: tuition costs are negligible and the student lives at home. In some of the independent cities which I have visited, about half the high school graduates enroll in the local junior college. At the end of two years about a third of those who enter transfer to the university or to one of the four-year state colleges scattered throughout the state. Clearly the California system provides relatively free higher education on an extremely flexible and broad basis. All this has been accomplished while the scholarly, scientific, and professional standards in the university have been maintained. In California one may say the amount and kind of instruction beyond the high school which a youth receives are fitted to his capacity and his desires.

Excellent as is the California system, it is not readily exportable to states where another pattern of post-high school education has developed earlier. In a good many states, however, the pattern is not fixed, and I suggest that in these states a good hard look be taken at the California system of higher education. An essential ingredient for the success of the junior college is the transfer program to the state university. This feature seems important to me if the junior college is to appeal to suburban parents; it provides the necessary status. If a system similar to that of California could be established in many states, I am inclined to believe the situation in suburban schools described in the next paragraphs could be alleviated at least partially.

The reader will recall that our system, if one can call it a system, provides for a relatively late decision as to whether a boy will try to enter a professional school, that is, undertake true university work. For the majority of parents in the heavily college-oriented suburb, however, this decision about their children is made when they are born. Kindergarten and first-grade teachers frequently hear such statements as, "I don't care what you do as long as Johnnie gets into Harvard." The parents are determined that at least the boys, regardless of ability, receive a degree from a college with high academic standards. The pressures mount from that time on through the grades, increasing in severity so that all three parties—school, child, and parent —are aware of the importance of college board examinations and the day when the fateful letter from the college admission office is due. I have heard from teachers and principals in some suburban schools that there is more evi-dence of breakdowns in health than ever before. Parents report children who experience nausea before coming to school each morning. So great are the pressures to succeed in school, to obtain top marks as well as to excel in extra-curricular activities, that I know of one community in which some parents actually have taken their children out of the public schools and placed them in private schools to lessen the degree of tension. This is a fact that critics of fads and frills and lack of academic standards in American public schools would find hard to believe.

To counteract the mental anguish of the child who lacks the academic ability to match his parents' ambitions, there must be a strong guidance department in the subur-ban schools. As early as the elementary grades the guidance officers ought to begin their program of realistic and frank discussions with parents about the *kind* of college to which their offspring might expect to gain admission. Standardized scholastic aptitude test results, classroom achievement, teacher estimate—these are all tools at the disposal of the guidance officer. Of course, no dogmatic statement can be made that a certain boy or girl will or will not be admitted to Yale or Vassar. Nevertheless, certainly by the sixth grade the guidance officers have ample evidence to give a rough estimate of the chances of admission to one of these institutions—even allowing for the possibility that a "late bloomer" is at hand. This frank discussion I am suggesting that would take place between counselors and parents includes a careful interpretation of standardized test results, tests of scholastic aptitude among them. These tests, together with teacher grades, are excellent predictors of future academic success. It is the parents' right to have access to any information used by the school in educational planning, and such information interpreted by trained guidance officers will assist the parents in aiming at realistic goals for their children.

I have said that the use of standardized aptitude tests may be of great assistance to the counselors in any type of school. They indicate a probability of a pupil's being able to carry without undue strain a certain academic burden. Looked at in another way, they indicate which students will take a short time to master academic work and which students will take a long time. One does not say a student cannot learn the material; one says his learning time is too long to warrant the time spent. This concept of time is useful and has implications for suburban schools, where most pupils, regardless of ability, must take academic elective subjects.

Our schools generally proceed under the assumption that the time devoted to the study of a particular subject will be constant for all pupils, but that achievement will vary. It is on the basis of this assumption that school people predict, for instance, that a slow pupil will be better off studying general mathematics than algebra. They are aware, generalizing from experience, that the slow pupil in one year of algebra will progress so slowly that his potential mastery of the subject in the time devoted to it will not warrant his taking the course. If, however, the assumption is made that achievement will be held constant, but that the time devoted to the study of a subject will vary according to student ability, one clearly has a different situation. The slow student may do one year's algebra in two years. Whether this is a worthwhile use of his time is another matter. In any case, I think this question might well be explored in suburban schools where college pressures are great. I might note that some proponents of teaching machines make this latter assumption; namely, that theoretically most if not all pupils through the use of machines will eventually reach the same degree of mastery of a given subject but that they will do so with varying degrees of speed. The fast student will obtain two or more A's in the length of time it takes the slow student to obtain one A!

What would be the minimum academic content of four years of study for the average pupil in grades 9 through 12? Required of all students, regardless of ability, should be four years of English composition and literature, at least three years of American history and social studies, and at least one year each of mathematics and science. As for the elective programs of the average students in suburban schools, I should be ready to assert that they should study as much mathematics, science, and social science as they can master without an undue strain. In the suburban community, most of these students will go to college somewhere, and through hard work some may follow professional careers.

We do not as yet have evidence enough to say what is the relation of aptitude for the study of a foreign language by the new methods to the other scholastic aptitudes. Time alone will tell. However, my guess would be that there will be some among the average students who have marked ability for languages. These pupils should be encouraged to take a four-year sequence of one modern foreign language. Other students who are not academically talented may show marked aptitude for another skill or group of skills. Their school programs should be tailored to their special set of aptitudes. To attempt to force those with such a wide divergence in specialized aptitudes into the program I have recommended for the academically talented would be a great mistake. Perhaps I should point out in this connection that in recent decades the number and diversity of semiprofessional and technical vocations for individuals with specialized talents has increased enormously. Career possibilities for the individual of limited or one-sided talents are manifold, and for many should bring satisfaction as well as the opportunity to do useful work. By contrast, the academically talented student has aptitudes that also may vary, but his cluster of abilities is such that a wide academic program is a profitable and rewarding experience.

It seems to me that there is merit in further experimentation with the presentation of the physical sciences at different levels of sophistication. As usually presented, physics and chemistry can hardly be handled by other than the academically talented unless one has special aptitude for science and mathematics. I know of some suburban schools where physics and chemistry are presented in ways that might almost be described as teaching *about* physical science instead of teaching physics and chemistry. The objection to such a diluted course is the danger of creating a delusion in the parents' or children's minds as to what has been taught. Above all, these courses must not be used by able pupils as an escape hatch from a stiff program of physics and chemistry.

I have noted the possibility of presenting algebra in two years rather than one for some pupils. Certainly one cannot throw out of court without examination all proposals which would involve a four-year sequence of study of mathematics in which the student in four years would reach only a point considerably below that reached by the academically talented in, say, two years. This approach is similar to that of the ungraded primary, a new development in the elementary school which allows fast pupils to do three years' work in two and very slow pupils to do the three years' work in four years.

## The Slow Learner

The programs of the students with less-than-average ability and little interest in academic work remain to be considered. In the type of school we are considering in this chapter, there will be relatively few whose aptitudes, reading abilities, and interests place them in this category. Yet few as they are, they may present a problem and a different kind of problem from that presented by the existence of the same group in another type of community. As a first consideration, what kinds of courses in the usual academic subjects can the below-average student master without an undue burden on his time?

Aside from required academic courses, there is considerable question about the value of additional academic elective courses for below-average students. Art and music flourish in many suburban schools, and one finds less able pupils in academic areas often taking numerous courses in art and music—partially, I suspect, to fill out their schedules. It is as difficult to find a suitable elective program for these students in suburban schools as elsewhere.

Suburban parents are unlikely to be interested in practical courses for their children—the kinds of courses that to my mind are appropriate for these slower-than-average students. This aversion to practical courses is particularly conspicuous in the heavily college-oriented suburb. For girls, courses in elementary bookkeeping and business arithmetic (often a repetition of elementary school arithmetic) have some attraction, and the wise counselor will recom-

mend them to girls without academic abilities. The courses
in stenography are not for the below-average student.
Some girls will wish to take a second year of typewriting;
I assume that at some point in their schooling all the boys
and girls will elect a course in personal typewriting. Home
economics courses are popular with the girls I have in mind.

The boys who have difficulty with their studies are
not so well off in the college-oriented suburban school as
are the girls. There are no vocational courses at a suitable
level except perhaps in area vocational schools that often
fail to attract suburban boys because of the unfortunate
stigma attached to them. It is usual to find the boys who
have great difficulty with their academic work studying
business law or business arithmetic or bookkeeping or continuing with the industrial arts courses in grades 10 through
12.

The fact that the adjective "business" is used lends
some respectability to courses that generally are designed
for students slower than those enrolled in algebra, for
example. The name attached to a course is all-important
in the suburban schools. One must weigh, of course, the
advantage of enrolling the student in the course where he
can succeed against the disadvantage of deluding him and
his parents to the effect that business arithmetic will make
him a corporation president!

To be sure, in one or two suburban high schools which
I know about, the industrial arts shops are well equipped,
and one can maintain that in the industrial arts programs,
if time enough is allowed for the work, a boy may develop
a competence in metal work, electrical work, or certain
types of woodworking which could be called vocational.
In contrast to this, however, one finds that the industrial
arts instructors are tied to a special philosophy of their
work which, to my mind, while satisfactory for the lower
grades, does not correspond to the realities of life for the
senior high school student. The courses often fail to interest

him. And clearly, unless a boy believes that what he is doing with his hands in the shops is likely to have significance in his later life, there will be little or no motivating effect from the practical course.

There is considerable literature written by the proponents of the industrial arts which sets forth the standard doctrine. This doctrine is that the objective of the practical work is not so much to acquaint a boy with how to use tools and handle materials as to give him a practical acquaintance with the industrial world. Industrial arts are seen as general education. To this end one finds in some industrial arts courses a short exposure to a great variety of crafts, running all the way from leather work to casting aluminum. No real skill is developed, but a bowing acquaintance with the manipulation of the physical objects is provided. The theory is that such exposure makes the boy a more knowledgeable citizen in our industrialized and urbanized society.

I have never seen any evidence to support this theory. In my view a knowledge of science and mathematics in addition to comprehension of the nature of our society provided in social science courses—in short, the required general education program—is more relevant to this purpose than work in the industrial arts. To divert the purpose of programs concerned with the development of manual skills to this general objective is, therefore, to deprive them of what value they might have for students whose academic abilities are below average. At the same time, to my mind, such an objective adds little or nothing to the value of these courses for the average or brighter-than-average student. Bear in mind that I do think industrial arts ought to be required of all students as part of general education in the junior high school years.

Like my recommendation for the large cities, I think every suburban high school should have an auto mechanics shop run by a skilled mechanic who is interested in developing skills in boys who will go to work immediately after graduation from high school. I suspect that the interest and motivation of more than one boy in suburban communities would have been saved if such a shop had been available. A slow learner will never become a skilled mechanic, but even if he only washes cars, he is likely to see a relevance between school and a future job. As a result, his interest may carry over to his academic work. I repeat my contention that the motivating factor of vocational work is a most important consideration in the education of many boys and girls.

Electronics shops are becoming increasingly popular, but the procedures called for in serious electronics work are not easy and there is considerable question as to their value to the students I am discussing. Nevertheless, in both these areas of auto mechanics and electronics I think the suburban school could do much more than at present. Tied in with continued training in a terminal program in a two-year college or technical institute, these courses in high school might well provide an excellent means of educating students with average or less-than-average ability. Needless to say, at present there is an ever-growing demand for technicians of all sorts, and even some of the least-gifted students may find it possible to qualify for the more routine among technical jobs.

Finally, it seems to me that the field of work experience holds great promise for below-average students in suburbs as well as other types of communities. Provided that the cooperation of local businessmen can be obtained, suburban schools might well do more with part-time schooling and part-time employment. Students spend half the day in school and half the day on the job. Whether suburban parents with their eyes on college would allow their offspring to enroll in work-experience programs is another but obviously important matter that, again, involves the whole question of good guidance.

It is a very unfortunate fact that false prestige implying a higher social status for those who have "attended" college constitutes a threat to improvements long overdue in educating our youth. That education beyond the high school is a *longer* education is no reason to regard it as a *better* education. Full-time education beyond high school is desirable only to the extent that it develops further the potentialities of the student. For the scientist, doctor, lawyer, and scholar, six years beyond high school is a minimum. For other occupations, shorter periods of time are justified. In some cases, termination of full-time education prior to high school graduation makes sense. Snobbery that equates the length of education with its value has placed in some areas, especially wealthy suburban communities, a stigma upon high school vocational education. This snobbery can well be held responsible for the misery and frustration of many suburban children whose academic talents do not qualify them for advanced academic work. Moreover such a view runs completely counter to our frontier-derived heritage of equality of status for all forms of honest labor. There has been too much talk of the "necessity" to go to college in order to get ahead. Qualities of leadership, perseverance, honesty, and common sense are not found solely on college campuses.

In closing this chapter, I should like to express the hope that the lighthouse suburban schools, often in the forefront of change, will tackle the problem of the average and below-average student. I am one who has been much concerned about the generally inadequate attention the bright student has received in American public education. But one must remember that half the population has below-average ability. As I have suggested more sharply in earlier chapters, much remains to be done for the bottom half.

# CHAPTER V

## Programs of Study in Certain Schools

It is easy to write books about what students should or should not study, the kind of discussion I have engaged in up to this point. Of course, there will always be someone to take a different point of view, and the result is likely to be a lively debate. Needless to say, the high school curriculum has been debated endlessly in the past few years. The difficulty has been that as delightful as are the arguments, very few people have any meaningful facts as to what actually is going on in the schools. National statistics about the number of students studying physics, for example, are meaningless because they throw together students of all abilities in schools of all descriptions. Meaningful facts, it seems to me, require compilations of statistics state by state, preferably school by school, and by the ability levels of the students.

Because of my interest in schools in the metropolitan areas, I thought it might be worthwhile to gather such meaningful data from several of the well-known metropolitan schools of limited comprehensiveness; that is, schools where college interests predominated and where as a result there was not the same variety of elective programs I found in the widely comprehensive high schools of my first report. Two of these are not suburban schools, but selective academic high schools located within large cities. What I was interested in were the actual high school programs taken by students of different abilities in schools where more than 50 per cent of the graduating class went on to college, where school expenditures were high, and where the averages of the scholastic aptitude scores of the students were higher than in most schools. Table 2 gives the results of an extensive investigation. The schools chosen were the Bronx High School of Science in New York City, Central High School in Philadelphia, Evanston Township High School, Evanston, Illinois, Great Neck High Schools (there are two), Great Neck, Long Island, Newton High School (a second school has since opened), Newton, Massachusetts, and Scarsdale High School, Scarsdale, New York. I am much indebted to the principals of these schools for their cooperation in gathering the data and for their permission to print the results. I am indebted as well to Educational Testing Service for processing the data.

The Bronx High School of Science is a selective academic high school in New York City. It admits students from all over the city but only on examination. This school and Central High School in Philadelphia are to be contrasted with most of the public high schools in the country in this respect. Whereas most public high schools are comprehensive in that they enroll all pupils of a given district whatever their abilities, these two schools are not comprehensive, since they admit only very bright students on the basis of competitive examinations. In the Bronx High School of Science, for example, among the students sampled the average I.Q. was about 135. One hundred per cent of the students go to college. I doubt that there is another secondary school in the nation—public or private—that is more highly selective in terms of academic talent. Naturally, in such a school motivation toward schoolwork is extremely high.

The other schools are in suburbs outside New York, Boston, and Chicago, and are comprehensive schools that enroll students of all abilities in the district. There are differences among the communities and consequent differences among the schools. In the sample of students taken, the average I.Q. score varies from a low of 110 to a high of 126 and the fraction of the high school graduates going to college varies from 64 to 91 per cent. These facts mean there is a wider spread of ability and interests in some of these schools than in others. One or two are located in predominantly "bedroom" communities in which the vast majority of the fathers are business and professional people who commute to the central city and whose children "must" go to college. The other communities have many families much lower on the socio-economic ladder with children whose ambitions are to find employment after graduation from high school.

One common denominator among the suburban schools, as well as the selective academic high schools in the cities, is that all are known for excellent teaching. At least the suburban schools are in economically favored communities that take a great interest in providing the best teachers they can afford. Evanston and Newton have received national attention as a result of their pioneering efforts in new educational techniques such as team teaching. Evanston tops the list of the public high schools in terms of the numbers of students participating in the Advanced Placement Program, and Newton is not far behind. In short, these schools are said by many to be representative of the lighthouse schools that point the way to excellence in public education.

Readers of my first report may recall the academic inventories I printed there from several widely comprehensive high schools; that is, schools with fewer than 50 per cent of the graduates going on to college. Those inventories included only the academic programs taken by the top 15 per cent of the students on a national basis. The present inventories include students of all abilities in the class of 1959, grouped according to scores on tests of scholastic aptitude. In addition, both academic and nonacademic courses have been included, so that the total programs can be looked at.

One point I should like to make very clear. The academic inventory is simply a quantitative account of the courses taken by students during their high school careers. It in no way attests to the quality of what goes on in the classroom. I should say, however, that it is a first step toward the assessment of quality. For example, I believe students with certain academic talents should study advanced mathematics. Therefore, I should like to know how many of the students with these talents are, in fact, taking advanced mathematics. These are educational policy matters that a board of education ought in my judgment to take an interest in. The public ought to know what subjects students are studying. Beyond this point, however, professional judgment is necessary to determine the exact content of the course and the quality of the learning experience. Laymen should not become involved in judging the effectiveness of teachers.

A few explanatory notes are in order. Different tests are used in the various schools, errors of measurement are always present, and the sample of students in some of the groupings is very small. Despite these limitations, the inventories present a reliable picture of what subjects students of various ability levels are taking in these schools. To assist in interpreting the meaning of I.Q. scores, one must remember that they are good predictors of *academic* success; they are measures of scholastic aptitude. When looking at the nonacademic subjects, one should not assume that a boy with a high I.Q. score would necessarily do well in shop or music, for example, or that a boy with a low I.Q. score would do well in these subjects for that matter. In short, the correlation between I.Q. scores and academic success is higher than between I.Q. scores and success in nonacademic courses.

In terms of the total picture of scholastic aptitude, it

is convenient to remember that on a national basis roughly 67 per cent of all students have scores falling between 85 and 115, with the average at 100. This means that about 16 per cent have scores above 115 and 16 per cent have scores below 85. In all these schools combined, the curve of ability is skewed to the right with the average considerably above the national mean of 100 and at least half the students with scores at 115 or above. In the Bronx High School of Science the average student is in the top 2 or 3 per cent on a national basis.

I should note that in the schools where fewer than the entire member of graduates were included in the inventory the sample was drawn on a random basis. The tables do not show an occasional course that enrolls very few students. Also, there was a scholastic aptitude category 74-and-below, but it is not included because these mentally retarded youngsters are so few in number in these schools. Finally, a zero in the tables should be read as none or less than 1 per cent; a dash means no students in the category and, therefore, not applicable.

To my mind these inventories are very interesting and deserve considerable study on the part of those concerned with secondary education in their own communities. But unless the reader is prepared to take the time to delve into the many figures in the tables, he might move on to my few general comments and observations, which begin below and are continued at the end of the chapter.

## Some Observations

The first observation is to me the most significant. A glance at most of the comparable figures for each of the schools shows considerable differences. These differences show up in the percentages of students going to college, in total number of courses taken in four years, and in the total academic and nonacademic courses taken. For example, in the

I.Q. category 115–129, the percentage of boys going to college varies from 84 to 100. With respect to total courses for the same students, the figures vary from 96 per cent taking twenty-six or more to no boys at all with so extensive a program. The reader may recall my recommendation of at least eighteen academic subjects, or 4.5 a year in grades 9 through 12 for this same group. The figure varies again from 100 per cent to no boys at all. Finally, the percentage of these same boys who take at least six non-academic subjects, or 1.5 a year, varies from 100 to 15 per cent. These are typical of the differences these inventories record. They are facts. One can proceed to make any value judgment he wishes about them. Are the policy decisions reflected in these facts good, are they bad, or does it make no difference? For example, a policy decision with a long history in many parts of the nation, especially with at least one state committee of the North Central Association in the Mid-West, is that four academic subjects per year is the load that students should carry. I frankly think this policy is poor, that five academic subjects a year are well within the grasp of bright students and constitute no threat to their health or welfare. This is the kind of issue readers might well ponder as they look at the tables.

In looking at the percentages going on to college, what strikes one first is the obviously high positive correlation between scholastic aptitude and college entrance in all the schools. Greater percentages of bright students go on to college than do percentages of slow students. For example, in Great Neck 56 per cent of the boys and 40 per cent of the girls in the I.Q. category 90–104 go to college, whereas 100 per cent of the boys and girls in the category 130 go to college. One would expect this kind of relationship, but what is astonishing is the fact that so many pupils from the average and below-average ability groups go on to higher education. Note that in Evanston and Newton there are students in the I.Q. category 75–89 who go to college.

## BRONX HIGH SCHOOL OF SCIENCE,
### *1959 Graduates: 780; Graduates in Sample:*

| I.Q. Groupings | 75–89 | | 90–104 | | 105–114 | | 115–129 | | 130 plus | | All IQ's | | |
|---|---|---|---|---|---|---|---|---|---|---|---|---|---|
| Boys—Girls | Boy | Girl | Boy | Girl | Boy | Girl | Boy | Girl | Boy | Girl | Boy | Girl | Total |
| Number | — | — | 1 | — | 5 | 1 | 26 | 15 | 224 | 109 | 256 | 125 | 381 |
| | | | | | (Figures are per cents) | | | | | | | | |
| In College | — | — | 100 | — | 100 | 100 | 100 | 100 | 100 | 99 | 100 | 99 | 100 |
| Other post–H.S. education | — | — | 0 | — | 0 | 0 | 0 | 0 | 0 | 0 | 0 | 0 | 0 |
| Employed | — | — | 0 | — | 0 | 0 | 0 | 0 | 0 | 0 | 0 | 0 | 0 |
| **Total Courses** | | | | | | | | | | | | | |
| 26 or more | — | — | 100 | — | 100 | 100 | 96 | 100 | 96 | 96 | 96 | 97 | 96 |
| 20 or more | — | — | 100 | — | 100 | 100 | 100 | 100 | 100 | 100 | 100 | 100 | 100 |
| **Total Academic** | | | | | | | | | | | | | |
| 18 or more | — | — | 100 | — | 100 | 100 | 100 | 100 | 99 | 97 | 99 | 98 | 98 |
| 12 or more | — | — | 100 | — | 100 | 100 | 100 | 100 | 100 | 100 | 100 | 100 | 100 |
| **Total Nonacademic** | | | | | | | | | | | | | |
| 10 or more | — | — | 0 | — | 0 | 0 | 0 | 0 | 0 | 0 | 0 | 0 | 0 |
| 6 or more | — | — | 100 | — | 100 | 100 | 100 | 100 | 100 | 100 | 100 | 100 | 100 |
| **English** | | | | | | | | | | | | | |
| At least 3 years | — | — | 100 | — | 100 | 100 | 100 | 100 | 100 | 100 | 100 | 100 | 100 |
| At least 4 years | — | — | 100 | — | 100 | 100 | 100 | 100 | 100 | 100 | 100 | 100 | 100 |
| **Social Studies** | | | | | | | | | | | | | |
| At least 3 years | — | — | 100 | — | 100 | 100 | 100 | 100 | 100 | 100 | 100 | 100 | 100 |
| At least 4 years | — | — | 100 | — | 100 | 100 | 100 | 100 | 100 | 100 | 100 | 100 | 100 |
| **Mathematics** | | | | | | | | | | | | | |
| At least 3 years | — | — | 100 | — | 100 | 100 | 100 | 100 | 100 | 97 | 100 | 98 | 99 |
| At least 4 years | — | — | 0 | — | 80 | 100 | 65 | 33 | 83 | 64 | 80 | 61 | 74 |
| **Science** | | | | | | | | | | | | | |
| At least 3 years | — | — | 100 | — | 100 | 100 | 100 | 100 | 100 | 100 | 100 | 100 | 100 |
| At least 4 years | — | — | 100 | — | 100 | 100 | 100 | 100 | 98 | 98 | 98 | 98 | 98 |
| **Foreign Language (Total)** | | | | | | | | | | | | | |
| At least 3 years | — | — | 100 | — | 100 | 100 | 100 | 100 | 99 | 100 | 99 | 100 | 99 |
| At least 4 years | — | — | 0 | — | 0 | 0 | 0 | 7 | 0 | 1 | 0 | 2 | 1 |
| **One Foreign Language** | | | | | | | | | | | | | |
| At least 3 years | — | — | 100 | — | 100 | 100 | 100 | 100 | 99 | 100 | 99 | 100 | 99 |
| At least 4 years | — | — | 0 | — | 0 | 0 | 0 | 0 | 0 | 0 | 0 | 0 | 0 |
| **Advanced Placement** | | | | | | | | | | | | | |
| English | — | — | 0 | — | 0 | 0 | 0 | 0 | 0 | 0 | 0 | 0 | 0 |
| Languages | — | — | 0 | — | 0 | 0 | 0 | 0 | 0 | 0 | 0 | 0 | 0 |
| Mathematics | — | — | 0 | — | 0 | 0 | 4 | 0 | 6 | 1 | 5 | 1 | 4 |
| Science | — | — | 0 | — | 0 | 0 | 8 | 0 | 7 | 5 | 7 | 4 | 6 |
| Social Studies | — | — | 0 | — | 0 | 0 | 0 | 0 | 0 | 0 | 0 | 0 | 0 |

# Academic Inventories
# New York City (Class of 1959—Grades 9–12)
## 381; Mean I.Q. of Sample: 135

| I.Q. Groupings | 75–89 | | 90–104 | | 105–114 | | 115–129 | | 130 plus | | All IQ.s | | |
|---|---|---|---|---|---|---|---|---|---|---|---|---|---|
| Boys—Girls | Boy | Girl | Boy | Girl | Boy | Girl | Boy | Girl | Boy | Girl | Boy | Girl | Total |
| Number | — | — | 1 | — | 5 | 1 | 26 | 15 | 224 | 109 | 256 | 125 | 381 |
| | | | | | (Figures are per cents) | | | | | | | | |
| **Physics** | | | | | | | | | | | | | |
| At least 1 year | — | — | 100 | — | 100 | 100 | 96 | 100 | 99 | 98 | 98 | 98 | 98 |
| **Combinations** | | | | | | | | | | | | | |
| At least 7 years sci. & math. | — | — | 100 | — | 100 | 100 | 100 | 100 | 99 | 97 | 99 | 98 | 99 |
| At least 7 years Eng. & soc. st. | — | — | 100 | — | 100 | 100 | 100 | 100 | 100 | 100 | 100 | 100 | 100 |
| At least 4 years tot. foreign language, 7 years Eng. & soc. st., 7 years math. and science | — | — | 0 | — | 0 | 0 | 0 | 7 | 0 | 1 | 0 | 2 | 1 |
| **Art** | | | | | | | | | | | | | |
| At least 1 year | — | — | 100 | — | 100 | 100 | 100 | 100 | 100 | 100 | 100 | 100 | 100 |
| At least 2 years | — | — | 0 | — | 0 | 0 | 4 | 53 | 5 | 22 | 5 | 26 | 12 |
| **Music** | | | | | | | | | | | | | |
| At least 1 year | — | — | 100 | — | 100 | 100 | 100 | 100 | 100 | 100 | 100 | 100 | 100 |
| At least 2 years | — | — | 0 | — | 0 | 0 | 0 | 0 | 0 | 0 | 0 | 0 | 0 |
| **Typing** | | | | | | | | | | | | | |
| At least 1 year | — | — | 0 | — | 0 | 0 | 0 | 0 | 0 | 0 | 0 | 0 | 0 |
| At least 2 years | — | — | 0 | — | 0 | 0 | 0 | 0 | 0 | 0 | 0 | 0 | 0 |
| **Business and Secretarial** | | | | | | | | | | | | | |
| At least 1 year | — | — | 0 | — | 0 | 0 | 0 | 0 | 0 | 0 | 0 | 0 | 0 |
| At least 2 years | — | — | 0 | — | 0 | 0 | 0 | 0 | 0 | 0 | 0 | 0 | 0 |
| **Shop (incl. mech. dwg.)** | | | | | | | | | | | | | |
| At least 1 year | — | — | 100 | — | 100 | 100 | 100 | 100 | 100 | 100 | 100 | 100 | 100 |
| At least 2 years | — | — | 0 | — | 0 | 0 | 8 | 0 | 7 | 0 | 7 | 0 | 4 |
| **Home Economics** | | | | | | | | | | | | | |
| At least 1 year | — | — | 0 | — | 0 | 0 | 0 | 0 | 0 | 0 | 0 | 0 | 0 |
| At least 2 years | — | — | 0 | — | 0 | 0 | 0 | 0 | 0 | 0 | 0 | 0 | 0 |
| **Physical Education** | | | | | | | | | | | | | |
| At least 3 years | — | — | 100 | — | 100 | 100 | 100 | 100 | 100 | 99 | 100 | 99 | 100 |
| At least 4 years | — | — | 100 | — | 100 | 100 | 100 | 100 | 99 | 99 | 99 | 99 | 99 |

TABLE 2 *(cont.)*:
# CENTRAL HIGH SCHOOL, *Philadelphia,*
## *1959 Graduates: 492; Graduates in Sample:*

| I.Q. Groupings | 75–89 | | 90–104 | | 105–114 | | 115–129 | | 130 plus | | All I.Q.'s | | |
|---|---|---|---|---|---|---|---|---|---|---|---|---|---|
| Boys—Girls Number | Boy — | Girl — | Boy 4 | Girl — | Boy 39 | Girl — | Boy 225 | Girl — | Boy 223 | Girl — | Boy 491 | Girl — | Total 491 |
| | | | | | (Figures are per cents) | | | | | | | | |
| In College | — | — | 50 | — | 72 | — | 88 | — | 92 | — | 88 | — | 88 |
| Other post–H.S. education | — | — | 0 | — | 5 | — | 0 | — | 0 | — | 0 | — | 1 |
| Employed | — | — | 50 | — | 15 | — | 8 | — | 5 | — | 0 | — | 8 |
| Total Courses | | | | | | | | | | | | | |
| 26 or more | — | — | 0 | — | 33 | — | 31 | — | 33 | — | 32 | — | 32 |
| 20 or more | — | — | 100 | — | 100 | — | 100 | — | 100 | — | 100 | — | 100 |
| Total Academic | | | | | | | | | | | | | |
| 18 or more | — | — | 0 | — | 10 | — | 7 | — | 26 | — | 16 | — | 16 |
| 12 or more | — | — | 100 | — | 100 | — | 100 | — | 100 | — | 100 | — | 100 |
| Total Nonacademic | | | | | | | | | | | | | |
| 10 or more | — | — | 50 | — | 33 | — | 34 | — | 28 | — | 31 | — | 31 |
| 6 or more | — | — | 100 | — | 100 | — | 99 | — | 100 | — | 99 | — | 99 |
| English | | | | | | | | | | | | | |
| At least 3 years | — | — | 100 | — | 100 | — | 100 | — | 100 | — | 100 | — | 100 |
| At least 4 years | — | — | 100 | — | 100 | — | 98 | — | 99 | — | 98 | — | 98 |
| Social Studies | | | | | | | | | | | | | |
| At least 3 years | — | — | 100 | — | 100 | — | 100 | — | 100 | — | 100 | — | 100 |
| At least 4 years | — | — | 0 | — | 8 | — | 9 | — | 6 | — | 7 | — | 7 |
| Mathematics | | | | | | | | | | | | | |
| At least 3 years | — | — | 100 | — | 97 | — | 96 | — | 99 | — | 98 | — | 98 |
| At least 4 years | — | — | 50 | — | 82 | — | 77 | — | 87 | — | 82 | — | 82 |
| Science | | | | | | | | | | | | | |
| At least 3 years | — | — | 0 | — | 82 | — | 69 | — | 81 | — | 75 | — | 75 |
| At least 4 years | — | — | 0 | — | 3 | — | 1 | — | 0 | — | 1 | — | 1 |
| Foreign Language (Total) | | | | | | | | | | | | | |
| At least 3 years | — | — | 0 | — | 26 | — | 35 | — | 60 | — | 45 | — | 45 |
| At least 4 years | — | — | 0 | — | 13 | — | 13 | — | 33 | — | 22 | — | 22 |
| One Foreign Language | | | | | | | | | | | | | |
| At least 3 years | — | — | 0 | — | 23 | — | 31 | — | 55 | — | 41 | — | 41 |
| At least 4 years | — | — | 0 | — | 10 | — | 10 | — | 26 | — | 17 | — | 17 |
| Advanced Placement | | | | | | | | | | | | | |
| English | — | — | 0 | — | 0 | — | 0 | — | 12 | — | 6 | — | 6 |
| Languages | — | — | 0 | — | 0 | — | 1 | — | 8 | — | 4 | — | 4 |
| Mathematics | — | — | 0 | — | 0 | — | 0 | — | 11 | — | 5 | — | 5 |
| Science | — | — | 0 | — | 0 | — | 0 | — | 5 | — | 2 | — | 2 |
| Social Studies | — | — | 0 | — | 0 | — | 0 | — | 7 | — | 3 | — | 3 |

# Academic Inventories
## Pennsylvania (Class of 1959—Grades 9–12)
### 491; Mean I.Q. of Sample: 128

| I.Q. Groupings | 75–89 | | 90–104 | | 105–114 | | 115–129 | | 130 plus | | All I.Q's | | |
|---|---|---|---|---|---|---|---|---|---|---|---|---|---|
| Boys—Girls<br>Number | Boy<br>— | Girl<br>— | Boy<br>4 | Girl<br>— | Boy<br>39 | Girl<br>— | Boy<br>225 | Girl<br>— | Boy<br>223 | Girl<br>— | Boy<br>491 | Girl<br>— | Total<br>491 |
| | | | | (Figures are per cents) | | | | | | | | | |
| **Physics** | | | | | | | | | | | | | |
| At least 1 year | — | — | 0 | — | 87 | — | 80 | — | 91 | — | 85 | — | 85 |
| **Combinations** | | | | | | | | | | | | | |
| At least 7 years sci. &<br>math. | — | — | 0 | — | 74 | — | 61 | — | 74 | — | 68 | — | 68 |
| At least 7 years Eng.<br>& soc. st. | — | — | 100 | — | 100 | — | 97 | — | 99 | — | 98 | — | 98 |
| At least 4 years tot.<br>foreign language,<br>7 years Eng. & soc.<br>st., 7 years math.<br>and science | — | — | 0 | — | 8 | — | 5 | — | 24 | — | 14 | — | 14 |
| **Art** | | | | | | | | | | | | | |
| At least 1 year | — | — | 100 | — | 97 | — | 98 | — | 100 | — | 99 | — | 99 |
| At least 2 years | — | — | 75 | — | 64 | — | 56 | — | 48 | — | 53 | — | 53 |
| **Music** | | | | | | | | | | | | | |
| At least 1 year | — | — | 100 | — | 100 | — | 98 | — | 99 | — | 99 | — | 99 |
| At least 2 years | — | — | 100 | — | 82 | — | 89 | — | 79 | — | 84 | — | 84 |
| **Typing** | | | | | | | | | | | | | |
| At least 1 year | — | — | 0 | — | 0 | — | 0 | — | 0 | — | 0 | — | 0 |
| At least 2 years | — | — | 0 | — | 0 | — | 0 | — | 0 | — | 0 | — | 0 |
| **Business and Secretarial** | | | | | | | | | | | | | |
| At least 1 year | — | — | 0 | — | 0 | — | 0 | — | 0 | — | 0 | — | 0 |
| At least 2 years | — | — | 0 | — | 0 | — | 0 | — | 0 | — | 0 | — | 0 |
| **Shop (incl. mech. dwg.)** | | | | | | | | | | | | | |
| At least 1 year | — | — | 25 | — | 36 | — | 28 | — | 28 | — | 29 | — | 29 |
| At least 2 years | — | — | 25 | — | 15 | — | 14 | — | 9 | — | 12 | — | 12 |
| **Home Economics** | | | | | | | | | | | | | |
| At least 1 year | — | — | 0 | — | 0 | — | 0 | — | 0 | — | 0 | — | 0 |
| At least 2 years | — | — | 0 | — | 0 | — | 0 | — | 0 | — | 0 | — | 0 |
| **Physical Education** | | | | | | | | | | | | | |
| At least 3 years | — | — | 100 | — | 100 | — | 100 | — | 100 | — | 100 | — | 100 |
| At least 4 years | — | — | 100 | — | 100 | — | 100 | — | 100 | — | 100 | — | 100 |

| I.Q. Groupings | 75–89 | | 90–104 | | 105–114 | | 115–129 | | 130 plus | | All I.Q.'s | | |
|---|---|---|---|---|---|---|---|---|---|---|---|---|---|
| Boys—Girls Number | Boy 13 | Girl 5 | Boy 27 | Girl 26 | Boy 43 | Girl 44 | Boy 47 | Girl 50 | Boy 27 | Girl 14 | Boy 157 | Girl 139 | Total 296 |
| | (Figures are per cents) | | | | | | | | | | | | |
| In College | 23 | 40 | 52 | 50 | 72 | 70 | 89 | 86 | 93 | 86 | 73 | 73 | 73 |
| Other post–H.S. education | 0 | 0 | 7 | 12 | 0 | 7 | 2 | 2 | 0 | 0 | 2 | 5 | 3 |
| Employed | 46 | 40 | 37 | 31 | 23 | 18 | 2 | 10 | 0 | 14 | 17 | 18 | 18 |
| **Total Courses** | | | | | | | | | | | | | |
| 26 or more | 0 | 20 | 0 | 8 | 0 | 11 | 0 | 24 | 22 | 21 | 4 | 17 | 10 |
| 20 or more | 77 | 100 | 67 | 92 | 93 | 93 | 91 | 96 | 93 | 100 | 87 | 95 | 91 |
| **Total Academic** | | | | | | | | | | | | | |
| 18 or more | 0 | 0 | 0 | 0 | 0 | 0 | 0 | 4 | 19 | 0 | 3 | 1 | 2 |
| 12 or more | 31 | 40 | 67 | 62 | 81 | 82 | 98 | 96 | 100 | 100 | 83 | 83 | 83 |
| **Total Nonacademic** | | | | | | | | | | | | | |
| 10 or more | 62 | 80 | 33 | 58 | 14 | 48 | 2 | 32 | 11 | 36 | 17 | 44 | 30 |
| 6 or more | 100 | 100 | 89 | 100 | 84 | 98 | 77 | 90 | 89 | 93 | 85 | 95 | 90 |
| **English** | | | | | | | | | | | | | |
| At least 3 years | 100 | 100 | 100 | 100 | 100 | 100 | 100 | 100 | 100 | 100 | 100 | 100 | 100 |
| At least 4 years | 100 | 100 | 100 | 10 | 100 | 100 | 100 | 100 | 100 | 100 | 100 | 100 | 100 |
| **Social Studies** | | | | | | | | | | | | | |
| At least 3 years | 31 | 40 | 48 | 62 | 58 | 70 | 70 | 72 | 59 | 86 | 58 | 70 | 64 |
| At least 4 years | 8 | 0 | 15 | 23 | 21 | 11 | 19 | 26 | 22 | 29 | 18 | 20 | 19 |
| **Mathematics** | | | | | | | | | | | | | |
| At least 3 years | 23 | 40 | 48 | 15 | 63 | 34 | 94 | 60 | 100 | 71 | 73 | 44 | 59 |
| At least 4 years | 8 | 0 | 15 | 4 | 42 | 18 | 70 | 20 | 74 | 36 | 48 | 17 | 34 |
| **Science** | | | | | | | | | | | | | |
| At least 3 years | 31 | 0 | 48 | 12 | 58 | 14 | 57 | 16 | 59 | 0 | 54 | 12 | 34 |
| At least 4 years | 8 | 0 | 15 | 0 | 19 | 0 | 28 | 2 | 22 | 0 | 20 | 1 | 11 |
| **Foreign Language (Total)** | | | | | | | | | | | | | |
| At least 3 years | 8 | 20 | 4 | 42 | 9 | 52 | 19 | 66 | 44 | 71 | 17 | 56 | 35 |
| At least 4 years | 0 | 20 | 4 | 12 | 0 | 20 | 4 | 50 | 30 | 57 | 7 | 33 | 19 |
| **One Foreign Language** | | | | | | | | | | | | | |
| At least 3 years | 8 | 20 | 0 | 31 | 9 | 41 | 17 | 52 | 37 | 50 | 15 | 43 | 28 |
| At least 4 years | 0 | 0 | 0 | 8 | 0 | 5 | 2 | 18 | 15 | 14 | 3 | 11 | 7 |
| **Advanced Placement** | | | | | | | | | | | | | |
| English | 0 | 0 | 0 | 0 | 0 | 0 | 0 | 4 | 15 | 14 | 3 | 3 | 3 |
| Languages | 0 | 0 | 0 | 0 | 2 | 0 | 2 | 4 | 15 | 7 | 4 | 2 | 3 |
| Mathematics | 0 | 0 | 0 | 0 | 0 | 0 | 4 | 2 | 37 | 7 | 8 | 1 | 5 |
| Science | 0 | 0 | 0 | 0 | 0 | 0 | 2 | 2 | 26 | 0 | 5 | 1 | 3 |
| Social Studies | 0 | 0 | 0 | 0 | 0 | 0 | 6 | 4 | 19 | 7 | 5 | 2 | 4 |

# Academic Inventories
## Evanston, Illinois (Class of 1959—Grades 9–12)
### Mean I.Q. of Sample: 114

| I.Q. Groupings | 75–89 | | 90–104 | | 105–114 | | 115–129 | | 130 plus | | All I.Q.'s | | |
|---|---|---|---|---|---|---|---|---|---|---|---|---|---|
| Boys—Girls Number | Boy 13 | Girl 5 | Boy 27 | Girl 26 | Boy 43 | Girl 44 | Boy 47 | Girl 50 | Boy 27 | Girl 14 | Boy 157 | Girl 139 | Total 296 |
| | | | | | (Figures are per cents) | | | | | | | | |
| **Physics** | | | | | | | | | | | | | |
| At least 1 year | 0 | 0 | 15 | 4 | 23 | 2 | 62 | 14 | 70 | 0 | 39 | 6 | 24 |
| **Combinations** | | | | | | | | | | | | | |
| At least 7 years sci. & math. | 0 | 0 | 15 | 4 | 44 | 5 | 49 | 6 | 56 | 7 | 39 | 5 | 23 |
| At least 7 years Eng. & soc. st. | 31 | 60 | 48 | 65 | 58 | 70 | 70 | 74 | 63 | 86 | 59 | 72 | 65 |
| At least 4 years tot. foreign language, 7 years Eng. & soc. st., 7 years math and science | 0 | 0 | 0 | 0 | 0 | 0 | 0 | 2 | 7 | 0 | 1 | 1 | 1 |
| **Art** | | | | | | | | | | | | | |
| At least 1 year | 77 | 60 | 89 | 58 | 81 | 64 | 68 | 68 | 74 | 50 | 77 | 63 | 70 |
| At least 2 years | 23 | 40 | 26 | 19 | 12 | 36 | 11 | 38 | 11 | 29 | 15 | 33 | 23 |
| **Music** | | | | | | | | | | | | | |
| At least 1 year | 54 | 80 | 33 | 54 | 26 | 64 | 32 | 44 | 30 | 57 | 32 | 55 | 43 |
| At least 2 years | 31 | 60 | 22 | 42 | 12 | 36 | 19 | 28 | 19 | 36 | 18 | 35 | 26 |
| **Typing** | | | | | | | | | | | | | |
| At least 1 year | 62 | 100 | 44 | 92 | 33 | 80 | 26 | 68 | 37 | 79 | 36 | 78 | 56 |
| At least 2 years | 8 | 20 | 4 | 46 | 0 | 23 | 0 | 16 | 0 | 0 | 1 | 22 | 11 |
| **Business and Secretarial** | | | | | | | | | | | | | |
| At least 1 year | 8 | 80 | 19 | 46 | 16 | 43 | 9 | 22 | 7 | 21 | 12 | 35 | 23 |
| At least 2 years | 0 | 20 | 0 | 23 | 7 | 23 | 4 | 12 | 0 | 14 | 3 | 18 | 10 |
| **Shop (incl. mech. dwg.)** | | | | | | | | | | | | | |
| At least 1 year | 85 | 0 | 56 | 0 | 51 | 0 | 45 | 0 | 33 | 0 | 50 | 0 | 26 |
| At least 2 years | 85 | 0 | 30 | 0 | 26 | 0 | 19 | 0 | 7 | 0 | 26 | 0 | 14 |
| **Home Economics** | | | | | | | | | | | | | |
| At least 1 year | 0 | 80 | 0 | 69 | 0 | 43 | 0 | 32 | 0 | 36 | 0 | 45 | 21 |
| At least 2 years | 0 | 40 | 0 | 31 | 0 | 9 | 0 | 0 | 0 | 0 | 0 | 10 | 5 |
| **Physical Education** | | | | | | | | | | | | | |
| At least 3 years | 100 | 100 | 81 | 96 | 100 | 98 | 94 | 94 | 93 | 93 | 94 | 96 | 95 |
| At least 4 years | 69 | 100 | 67 | 77 | 84 | 89 | 79 | 84 | 78 | 79 | 77 | 84 | 80 |

| I.Q. Groupings | 75–89 | | 90–104 | | 105–114 | | 115–129 | | 130 plus | | All I.Q.'s | | |
|---|---|---|---|---|---|---|---|---|---|---|---|---|---|
| Boys—Girls | Boy | Girl | Boy | Girl | Boy | Girl | Boy | Girl | Boy | Girl | Boy | Girl | Total |
| Number | 1 | 6 | 27 | 25 | 43 | 59 | 65 | 57 | 12 | 5 | 148 | 152 | 300 |
| | | | | | (Figures are per cents) | | | | | | | | |
| In College | 0 | 0 | 56 | 40 | 91 | 81 | 94 | 89 | 100 | 100 | 86 | 75 | 80 |
| Other post–H.S. education | 0 | 0 | 15 | 24 | 2 | 10 | 3 | 9 | 0 | 0 | 5 | 11 | 8 |
| Employed | 100 | 100 | 22 | 36 | 0 | 6 | 3 | 2 | 0 | 0 | 6 | 13 | 10 |
| **Total Courses** | | | | | | | | | | | | | |
| 26 or more | 0 | 0 | 0 | 0 | 0 | 0 | 0 | 4 | 8 | 0 | 1 | 1 | 1 |
| 20 or more | 0 | 33 | 44 | 76 | 84 | 98 | 88 | 95 | 100 | 100 | 79 | 91 | 85 |
| **Total Academic** | | | | | | | | | | | | | |
| 18 or more | 0 | 0 | 0 | 4 | 28 | 34 | 52 | 53 | 83 | 80 | 38 | 36 | 37 |
| 12 or more | 100 | 17 | 63 | 68 | 98 | 95 | 98 | 96 | 100 | 100 | 92 | 88 | 90 |
| **Total Nonacademic** | | | | | | | | | | | | | |
| 10 or more | 0 | 17 | 7 | 20 | 2 | 7 | 0 | 0 | 0 | 0 | 2 | 7 | 4 |
| 6 or more | 100 | 100 | 67 | 88 | 30 | 56 | 15 | 33 | 8 | 0 | 29 | 53 | 41 |
| **English** | | | | | | | | | | | | | |
| At least 3 years | 100 | 100 | 100 | 100 | 100 | 100 | 100 | 100 | 100 | 100 | 100 | 100 | 100 |
| At least 4 years | 100 | 100 | 100 | 100 | 100 | 100 | 100 | 100 | 100 | 100 | 100 | 100 | 100 |
| **Social Studies** | | | | | | | | | | | | | |
| At least 3 years | 100 | 100 | 100 | 100 | 100 | 100 | 100 | 100 | 100 | 100 | 100 | 100 | 100 |
| At least 4 years | 100 | 100 | 96 | 100 | 98 | 97 | 98 | 96 | 100 | 100 | 98 | 97 | 98 |
| **Mathematics** | | | | | | | | | | | | | |
| At least 3 years | 0 | 0 | 37 | 32 | 93 | 51 | 95 | 84 | 100 | 100 | 84 | 60 | 72 |
| At least 4 years | 0 | 0 | 19 | 4 | 51 | 14 | 69 | 18 | 75 | 60 | 55 | 14 | 34 |
| **Science** | | | | | | | | | | | | | |
| At least 3 years | 0 | 0 | 15 | 4 | 74 | 29 | 80 | 35 | 92 | 60 | 67 | 27 | 47 |
| At least 4 years | 0 | 0 | 7 | 0 | 33 | 3 | 62 | 0 | 75 | 20 | 44 | 2 | 23 |
| **Foreign Language (Total)** | | | | | | | | | | | | | |
| At least 3 years | 0 | 0 | 0 | 24 | 26 | 54 | 35 | 81 | 42 | 80 | 26 | 58 | 42 |
| At least 4 years | 0 | 0 | 0 | 16 | 5 | 39 | 12 | 61 | 17 | 80 | 8 | 43 | 26 |
| **One Foreign Language** | | | | | | | | | | | | | |
| At least 3 years | 0 | 0 | 0 | 12 | 21 | 42 | 28 | 72 | 42 | 60 | 22 | 47 | 35 |
| At least 4 years | 0 | 0 | 0 | 0 | 0 | 22 | 6 | 46 | 8 | 40 | 3 | 27 | 15 |
| **Advanced Placement** | | | | | | | | | | | | | |
| English | 0 | 0 | 0 | 0 | 0 | 0 | 0 | 0 | 0 | 0 | 0 | 0 | 0 |
| Languages | 0 | 0 | 0 | 0 | 0 | 0 | 0 | 0 | 0 | 0 | 0 | 0 | 0 |
| Mathematics | 0 | 0 | 0 | 0 | 0 | 0 | 0 | 0 | 0 | 0 | 0 | 0 | 0 |
| Science | 0 | 0 | 0 | 0 | 0 | 0 | 0 | 0 | 0 | 0 | 0 | 0 | 0 |
| Social Studies | 0 | 0 | 0 | 0 | 0 | 0 | 0 | 0 | 0 | 0 | 0 | 0 | 0 |

## Academic Inventories
### Great Neck, New York (Class of 1959—Grades 9–12)
#### Mean I.Q. of Sample: 114

| I.Q. Groupings | 75–89 | | 90–104 | | 105–114 | | 115–129 | | 130 plus | | All I.Q.'s | | |
|---|---|---|---|---|---|---|---|---|---|---|---|---|---|
| Boys—Girls<br>Number | Boy<br>1 | Girl<br>6 | Boy<br>27 | Girl<br>25 | Boy<br>43 | Girl<br>59 | Boy<br>65 | Girl<br>57 | Boy<br>12 | Girl<br>5 | Boy<br>148 | Girl<br>152 | Total<br>300 |
| | | | | | (Figures are per cents) | | | | | | | | |
| **Physics** | | | | | | | | | | | | | |
| At least 1 year | 0 | 0 | 22 | 0 | 40 | 3 | 69 | 5 | 100 | 60 | 54 | 5 | 29 |
| **Combinations** | | | | | | | | | | | | | |
| At least 7 years sci. & math. | 0 | 0 | 7 | 0 | 51 | 3 | 74 | 11 | 83 | 60 | 55 | 7 | 31 |
| At least 7 years Eng. & soc. st. | 100 | 100 | 100 | 100 | 100 | 100 | 100 | 100 | 100 | 100 | 100 | 100 | 100 |
| At least 4 years tot. foreign language, 7 years Eng. & soc. st., 7 years math. and science | 0 | 0 | 0 | 0 | 5 | 2 | 12 | 9 | 8 | 40 | 7 | 5 | 6 |
| **Art** | | | | | | | | | | | | | |
| At least 1 year | 0 | 17 | 19 | 32 | 16 | 44 | 6 | 53 | 8 | 40 | 11 | 44 | 28 |
| At least 2 years | 0 | 17 | 11 | 24 | 0 | 20 | 0 | 18 | 0 | 20 | 2 | 20 | 11 |
| **Music** | | | | | | | | | | | | | |
| At least 1 year | 0 | 0 | 26 | 44 | 23 | 59 | 20 | 44 | 33 | 20 | 23 | 47 | 35 |
| At least 2 years | 0 | 0 | 11 | 12 | 16 | 17 | 8 | 19 | 17 | 0 | 11 | 16 | 14 |
| **Typing** | | | | | | | | | | | | | |
| At least 1 year | 0 | 83 | 19 | 72 | 23 | 46 | 12 | 47 | 33 | 20 | 18 | 51 | 35 |
| At least 2 years | 0 | 17 | 0 | 28 | 0 | 5 | 0 | 0 | 0 | 0 | 0 | 7 | 4 |
| **Business and Secretarial** | | | | | | | | | | | | | |
| At least 1 year | 100 | 83 | 44 | 68 | 47 | 41 | 29 | 40 | 25 | 20 | 37 | 46 | 42 |
| At least 2 years | 0 | 67 | 19 | 56 | 23 | 24 | 15 | 12 | 0 | 0 | 17 | 26 | 21 |
| **Shop (incl. mech. dwg.)** | | | | | | | | | | | | | |
| At least 1 year | 100 | 0 | 81 | 0 | 49 | 2 | 48 | 2 | 33 | 0 | 53 | 1 | 27 |
| At least 2 years | 100 | 0 | 63 | 0 | 28 | 0 | 15 | 0 | 17 | 0 | 28 | 0 | 14 |
| **Home Economics** | | | | | | | | | | | | | |
| At least 1 year | 0 | 100 | 4 | 56 | 0 | 32 | 2 | 21 | 0 | 20 | 1 | 34 | 18 |
| At least 2 years | 0 | 83 | 0 | 24 | 0 | 12 | 0 | 5 | 0 | 0 | 0 | 14 | 7 |
| **Physical Education** | | | | | | | | | | | | | |
| At least 3 years | 0 | 0 | 0 | 0 | 0 | 0 | 0 | 0 | 0 | 0 | 0 | 0 | 0 |
| At least 4 years | 0 | 0 | 0 | 0 | 0 | 0 | 0 | 0 | 0 | 0 | 0 | 0 | 0 |

| I.Q. Groupings | 75–89 | | 90–104 | | 105–114 | | 115–129 | | 130 plus | | All I.Q.'s | | |
|---|---|---|---|---|---|---|---|---|---|---|---|---|---|
| Boys—Girls Number | Boy 12 | Girl 12 | Boy 39 | Girl 68 | Boy 70 | Girl 80 | Boy 69 | Girl 77 | Boy 6 | Girl 4 | Boy 198 | Girl 241 | Total 439 |
| | | | | | (Figures are per cents) | | | | | | | | |
| In College | 8 | 8 | 59 | 26 | 69 | 70 | 84 | 84 | 100 | 100 | 69 | 60 | 64 |
| Other post–H.S. education | 25 | 33 | 10 | 25 | 17 | 13 | 7 | 9 | 0 | 0 | 12 | 16 | 14 |
| Employed | 50 | 58 | 13 | 37 | 3 | 15 | 4 | 4 | 0 | 0 | 9 | 20 | 15 |
| Total Courses | | | | | | | | | | | | | |
| 26 or more | 33 | 33 | 15 | 44 | 24 | 41 | 35 | 55 | 50 | 75 | 28 | 46 | 38 |
| 20 or more | 92 | 100 | 97 | 99 | 96 | 100 | 97 | 100 | 100 | 100 | 96 | 100 | 98 |
| Total Academic | | | | | | | | | | | | | |
| 18 or more | 0 | 17 | 33 | 21 | 63 | 56 | 84 | 77 | 100 | 100 | 61 | 51 | 56 |
| 12 or more | 83 | 75 | 100 | 94 | 100 | 99 | 100 | 100 | 100 | 100 | 99 | 97 | 98 |
| Total Nonacademic | | | | | | | | | | | | | |
| 10 or more | 83 | 75 | 23 | 57 | 6 | 36 | 13 | 14 | 17 | 0 | 17 | 37 | 28 |
| 6 or more | 100 | 100 | 85 | 96 | 81 | 89 | 64 | 87 | 67 | 50 | 77 | 90 | 84 |
| English | | | | | | | | | | | | | |
| At least 3 years | 100 | 100 | 100 | 100 | 100 | 100 | 100 | 100 | 100 | 100 | 100 | 100 | 100 |
| At least 4 years | 100 | 100 | 100 | 100 | 99 | 100 | 100 | 100 | 100 | 100 | 99 | 100 | 100 |
| Social Studies | | | | | | | | | | | | | |
| At least 3 years | 100 | 100 | 100 | 97 | 96 | 94 | 97 | 100 | 100 | 100 | 97 | 97 | 97 |
| At least 4 years | 83 | 100 | 74 | 87 | 56 | 75 | 49 | 66 | 33 | 75 | 59 | 77 | 69 |
| Mathematics | | | | | | | | | | | | | |
| At least 3 years | 17 | 17 | 74 | 24 | 96 | 65 | 100 | 88 | 100 | 100 | 87 | 59 | 72 |
| At least 4 years | 8 | 8 | 44 | 3 | 57 | 15 | 72 | 21 | 100 | 75 | 58 | 14 | 34 |
| Science | | | | | | | | | | | | | |
| At least 3 years | 67 | 8 | 72 | 31 | 74 | 35 | 70 | 44 | 67 | 50 | 72 | 36 | 52 |
| At least 4 years | 8 | 0 | 8 | 12 | 29 | 13 | 45 | 8 | 17 | 0 | 28 | 10 | 18 |
| Foreign Language (Total) | | | | | | | | | | | | | |
| At least 3 years | 0 | 25 | 44 | 41 | 80 | 76 | 78 | 87 | 100 | 100 | 67 | 68 | 67 |
| At least 4 years | 0 | 8 | 23 | 29 | 40 | 65 | 49 | 81 | 67 | 100 | 38 | 58 | 49 |
| One Foreign Language | | | | | | | | | | | | | |
| At least 3 years | 0 | 8 | 31 | 26 | 59 | 51 | 67 | 64 | 67 | 100 | 52 | 47 | 49 |
| At least 4 years | 0 | 0 | 10 | 9 | 11 | 13 | 23 | 26 | 17 | 75 | 15 | 16 | 15 |
| Advanced Placement | | | | | | | | | | | | | |
| English | 0 | 0 | 0 | 0 | 0 | 0 | 3 | 6 | 33 | 75 | 2 | 3 | 3 |
| Languages | 0 | 0 | 0 | 0 | 1 | 0 | 7 | 4 | 33 | 25 | 4 | 2 | 3 |
| Mathematics | 0 | 0 | 0 | 0 | 0 | 0 | 10 | 0 | 50 | 25 | 5 | 0 | 3 |
| Science | 0 | 0 | 0 | 0 | 0 | 0 | 0 | 1 | 33 | 25 | 1 | 1 | 1 |
| Social Studies | 0 | 0 | 0 | 0 | 0 | 0 | 3 | 0 | 0 | 25 | 1 | 0 | 1 |

## *Academic Inventories*
### *Newton, Massachusetts (Class of 1959—Grades 9–12)*
*439; Mean I.Q. of Sample: 110*

| I.Q. Groupings | 75–89 | | 90–104 | | 105–114 | | 115–129 | | 130 plus | | All I.Q.'s | | |
|---|---|---|---|---|---|---|---|---|---|---|---|---|---|
| Boys—Girls Number | Boy 12 | Girl 12 | Boy 39 | Girl 68 | Boy 70 | Girl 80 | Boy 69 | Girl 77 | Boy 6 | Girl 4 | Boy 198 | Girl 241 | Total 439 |
| | | | | | (Figures are per cents) | | | | | | | | |
| **Physics** | | | | | | | | | | | | | |
| At least 1 year | 8 | 0 | 26 | 1 | 41 | 1 | 55 | 3 | 67 | 25 | 41 | 2 | 20 |
| **Combinations** | | | | | | | | | | | | | |
| At least 7 years sci. & math. | 17 | 0 | 38 | 7 | 51 | 13 | 59 | 14 | 67 | 50 | 49 | 12 | 29 |
| At least 7 years Eng. & soc. st. | 100 | 100 | 100 | 97 | 96 | 94 | 97 | 100 | 100 | 100 | 97 | 97 | 97 |
| At least 4 years tot. foreign language, 7 years Eng. & soc. st., 7 years math. and science | 0 | 0 | 15 | 3 | 17 | 5 | 16 | 10 | 33 | 50 | 16 | 7 | 11 |
| **Art** | | | | | | | | | | | | | |
| At least 1 year | 25 | 33 | 13 | 25 | 7 | 26 | 9 | 31 | 17 | 50 | 11 | 28 | 20 |
| At least 2 years | 17 | 25 | 5 | 9 | 1 | 14 | 4 | 12 | 0 | 25 | 4 | 12 | 9 |
| **Music** | | | | | | | | | | | | | |
| At least 1 year | 17 | 25 | 31 | 43 | 27 | 50 | 35 | 60 | 50 | 50 | 30 | 50 | 41 |
| At least 2 years | 17 | 8 | 10 | 22 | 11 | 31 | 16 | 36 | 33 | 25 | 14 | 29 | 22 |
| **Typing** | | | | | | | | | | | | | |
| At least 1 year | 42 | 75 | 49 | 71 | 43 | 64 | 51 | 56 | 17 | 0 | 45 | 63 | 55 |
| At least 2 years | 0 | 33 | 5 | 35 | 0 | 11 | 1 | 3 | 0 | 0 | 2 | 16 | 10 |
| **Business and Secretarial** | | | | | | | | | | | | | |
| At least 1 year | 92 | 83 | 36 | 53 | 21 | 24 | 13 | 9 | 0 | 0 | 26 | 30 | 28 |
| At least 2 years | 75 | 67 | 28 | 50 | 4 | 11 | 3 | 1 | 0 | 0 | 14 | 22 | 18 |
| **Shop (incl. mech. dwg.)** | | | | | | | | | | | | | |
| At least 1 year | 83 | 0 | 51 | 4 | 56 | 5 | 41 | 3 | 33 | 0 | 51 | 4 | 25 |
| At least 2 years | 58 | 0 | 26 | 0 | 29 | 3 | 14 | 1 | 17 | 0 | 25 | 1 | 12 |
| **Home Economics** | | | | | | | | | | | | | |
| At least 1 year | 67 | 83 | 18 | 66 | 16 | 56 | 10 | 36 | 17 | 50 | 18 | 54 | 38 |
| At least 2 years | 33 | 58 | 8 | 31 | 3 | 15 | 0 | 9 | 0 | 25 | 5 | 20 | 13 |
| **Physical Education** | | | | | | | | | | | | | |
| At least 3 years | 92 | 83 | 95 | 94 | 96 | 95 | 88 | 94 | 100 | 75 | 93 | 93 | 93 |
| At least 4 years | 75 | 67 | 85 | 84 | 89 | 86 | 74 | 87 | 100 | 50 | 82 | 84 | 83 |

| I.Q. Groupings | 75–89 | | 90–104 | | 105–114 | | 115–129 | | 130 plus | | All I.Q.'s | | |
|---|---|---|---|---|---|---|---|---|---|---|---|---|---|
| Boys—Girls Number | Boy — | Girl — | Boy 4 | Girl 4 | Boy 13 | Girl 25 | Boy 56 | Girl 56 | Boy 57 | Girl 60 | Boy 130 | Girl 145 | Total 275 |
| | | | | | (Figures are per cents) | | | | | | | | |
| In College | — | — | 50 | 75 | 85 | 76 | 89 | 95 | 96 | 97 | 91 | 92 | 91 |
| Other post–H.S. education | — | — | 0 | 0 | 8 | 4 | 5 | 2 | 0 | 2 | 3 | 2 | 3 |
| Employed | — | — | 0 | 0 | 0 | 12 | 0 | 0 | 0 | 0 | 1 | 3 | 2 |
| **Total Courses** | | | | | | | | | | | | | |
| 26 or more | — | — | 0 | 0 | 8 | 8 | 11 | 14 | 26 | 40 | 17 | 23 | 20 |
| 20 or more | — | — | 75 | 75 | 92 | 92 | 98 | 98 | 100 | 100 | 98 | 97 | 97 |
| **Total Academic** | | | | | | | | | | | | | |
| 18 or more | — | — | 25 | 0 | 0 | 16 | 23 | 54 | 54 | 80 | 35 | 57 | 46 |
| 12 or more | — | — | 75 | 75 | 92 | 92 | 96 | 100 | 100 | 100 | 97 | 98 | 97 |
| **Total Nonacademic** | | | | | | | | | | | | | |
| 10 or more | — | — | 0 | 0 | 8 | 24 | 7 | 11 | 9 | 2 | 8 | 9 | 8 |
| 6 or more | — | — | 75 | 100 | 100 | 92 | 93 | 80 | 89 | 85 | 92 | 85 | 88 |
| **English** | | | | | | | | | | | | | |
| At least 3 years | — | — | 100 | 100 | 100 | 100 | 100 | 100 | 100 | 100 | 100 | 100 | 100 |
| At least 4 years | — | — | 100 | 100 | 100 | 100 | 100 | 100 | 100 | 100 | 100 | 100 | 100 |
| **Social Studies** | | | | | | | | | | | | | |
| At least 3 years | — | — | 100 | 100 | 100 | 92 | 98 | 96 | 100 | 100 | 99 | 97 | 98 |
| At least 4 years | — | — | 75 | 50 | 62 | 72 | 27 | 41 | 28 | 23 | 32 | 39 | 36 |
| **Mathematics** | | | | | | | | | | | | | |
| At least 3 years | — | — | 25 | 50 | 85 | 44 | 93 | 73 | 98 | 97 | 92 | 77 | 84 |
| At least 4 years | — | — | 0 | 0 | 46 | 4 | 80 | 30 | 86 | 37 | 77 | 28 | 51 |
| **Science** | | | | | | | | | | | | | |
| At least 3 years | — | — | 25 | 0 | 38 | 0 | 48 | 7 | 67 | 17 | 55 | 10 | 31 |
| At least 4 years | — | — | 0 | 0 | 0 | 0 | 13 | 0 | 30 | 7 | 18 | 3 | 10 |
| **Foreign Language (Total)** | | | | | | | | | | | | | |
| At least 3 years | — | — | 25 | 25 | 8 | 80 | 45 | 93 | 84 | 100 | 58 | 92 | 76 |
| At least 4 years | — | — | 25 | 0 | 0 | 52 | 16 | 89 | 35 | 93 | 23 | 82 | 54 |
| **One Foreign Language** | | | | | | | | | | | | | |
| At least 3 years | — | — | 25 | 0 | 8 | 28 | 41 | 71 | 65 | 95 | 48 | 72 | 60 |
| At least 4 years | — | — | 0 | 0 | 0 | 4 | 4 | 32 | 11 | 62 | 6 | 39 | 23 |
| **Advanced Placement** | | | | | | | | | | | | | |
| English | — | — | 0 | 0 | 0 | 0 | 0 | 0 | 11 | 15 | 5 | 6 | 5 |
| Languages | — | — | 0 | 0 | 0 | 0 | 0 | 4 | 5 | 17 | 2 | 8 | 5 |
| Mathematics | — | — | 0 | 0 | 0 | 0 | 0 | 0 | 21 | 12 | 9 | 5 | 7 |
| Science | — | — | 0 | 0 | 0 | 0 | 2 | 5 | 12 | 5 | 6 | 4 | 5 |
| Social Studies | — | — | 0 | 0 | 0 | 0 | 0 | 0 | 9 | 8 | 4 | 3 | 4 |

## Academic Inventories
### Scarsdale, New York (Class of 1959—Grades 9–12)
275; Mean I.Q. of Sample: 126

| I.Q. Groupings | 75–89 | | 90–104 | | 105–114 | | 115–129 | | 130 plus | | All I.Q.'s | | |
|---|---|---|---|---|---|---|---|---|---|---|---|---|---|
| Boys—Girls Number | Boy — | Girl — | Boy 4 | Girl 4 | Boy 13 | Girl 25 | Boy 56 | Girl 56 | Boy 57 | Girl 60 | Boy 130 | Girl 145 | Total 275 |
| | | | | | (Figures are per cents) | | | | | | | | |
| **Physics** | | | | | | | | | | | | | |
| At least 1 year | — | — | 25 | 0 | 46 | 0 | 61 | 4 | 84 | 12 | 68 | 6 | 36 |
| **Combinations** | | | | | | | | | | | | | |
| At least 7 years sci. & math. | — | — | 0 | 0 | 31 | 0 | 41 | 2 | 65 | 10 | 49 | 5 | 26 |
| At least 7 years Eng. & soc. st. | — | — | 100 | 100 | 100 | 96 | 100 | 96 | 100 | 100 | 100 | 98 | 99 |
| At least 4 years tot. foreign language, 7 years Eng. & soc. st., 7 years math. and science | — | — | 0 | 0 | 0 | 0 | 4 | 2 | 18 | 8 | 9 | 4 | 7 |
| **Art** | | | | | | | | | | | | | |
| At least 1 year | — | — | 25 | 50 | 15 | 12 | 7 | 25 | 4 | 27 | 7 | 24 | 16 |
| At least 2 years | — | — | 25 | 0 | 8 | 4 | 2 | 18 | 2 | 3 | 3 | 7 | 5 |
| **Music** | | | | | | | | | | | | | |
| At least 1 year | — | — | 0 | 25 | 38 | 24 | 27 | 21 | 23 | 28 | 25 | 25 | 25 |
| At least 2 years | — | — | 0 | 25 | 31 | 12 | 18 | 4 | 14 | 13 | 17 | 10 | 13 |
| **Typing** | | | | | | | | | | | | | |
| At least 1 year | — | — | 0 | 25 | 0 | 44 | 5 | 14 | 4 | 5 | 4 | 16 | 10 |
| At least 2 years | — | — | 0 | 0 | 0 | 8 | 0 | 0 | 0 | 0 | 0 | 1 | 1 |
| **Business and Secretarial** | | | | | | | | | | | | | |
| At least 1 year | — | — | 100 | 25 | 46 | 40 | 9 | 14 | 4 | 5 | 13 | 15 | 14 |
| At least 2 years | — | — | 50 | 0 | 8 | 24 | 5 | 9 | 0 | 0 | 5 | 8 | 6 |
| **Shop (incl. mech. dwg.)** | | | | | | | | | | | | | |
| At least 1 year | — | — | 25 | 0 | 23 | 0 | 32 | 0 | 18 | 0 | 25 | 0 | 12 |
| At least 2 years | — | — | 0 | 0 | 8 | 0 | 9 | 0 | 5 | 0 | 7 | 0 | 3 |
| **Home Economics** | | | | | | | | | | | | | |
| At least 1 year | — | — | 0 | 50 | 0 | 20 | 0 | 11 | 0 | 10 | 0 | 13 | 7 |
| At least 2 years | — | — | 0 | 0 | 0 | 8 | 0 | 2 | 0 | 0 | 0 | 2 | 1 |
| **Physical Education** | | | | | | | | | | | | | |
| At least 3 years | — | — | 100 | 100 | 100 | 100 | 100 | 100 | 100 | 100 | 100 | 100 | 100 |
| At least 4 years | — | — | 100 | 100 | 100 | 100 | 100 | 100 | 100 | 100 | 100 | 100 | 100 |

| I.Q. Groupings | 75–89 | | 90–104 | | 105–114 | | 115–129 | | 130 plus | | All I.Q.'s | | |
|---|---|---|---|---|---|---|---|---|---|---|---|---|---|
| Boys—Girls Number | Boy 26 | Girl 23 | Boy 102 | Girl 123 | Boy 213 | Girl 209 | Boy 488 | Girl 255 | Boy 549 | Girl 192 | Boy 1378 | Girl 802 | Total 2180 |
| | | | | | (Figures are per cents) | | | | | | | | |
| In College | 15 | 13 | 56 | 36 | 76 | 74 | 89 | 89 | 96 | 97 | 86 | 77 | 83 |
| Other post–H.S. education | 12 | 17 | 11 | 21 | 8 | 10 | 2 | 5 | 0 | 1 | 3 | 8 | 5 |
| Employed | 50 | 65 | 24 | 35 | 8 | 13 | 5 | 4 | 2 | 1 | 7 | 12 | 9 |
| Total Courses | | | | | | | | | | | | | |
| 26 or more | 15 | 22 | 7 | 26 | 17 | 20 | 25 | 31 | 57 | 70 | 35 | 36 | 36 |
| 20 or more | 81 | 83 | 75 | 92 | 93 | 97 | 97 | 98 | 100 | 100 | 95 | 97 | 96 |
| Total Academic | | | | | | | | | | | | | |
| 18 or more | 0 | 9 | 15 | 12 | 31 | 33 | 30 | 53 | 60 | 84 | 40 | 48 | 43 |
| 12 or more | 58 | 52 | 80 | 81 | 95 | 93 | 99 | 98 | 100 | 100 | 97 | 94 | 96 |
| Total Nonacademic | | | | | | | | | | | | | |
| 10 or more | 69 | 61 | 22 | 48 | 12 | 29 | 19 | 13 | 13 | 3 | 17 | 21 | 18 |
| 6 or more | 100 | 100 | 81 | 95 | 77 | 82 | 80 | 75 | 96 | 91 | 86 | 84 | 86 |
| English | | | | | | | | | | | | | |
| At least 3 years | 100 | 100 | 100 | 100 | 100 | 100 | 100 | 100 | 100 | 100 | 100 | 100 | 100 |
| At least 4 years | 100 | 100 | 100 | 100 | 100 | 100 | 99 | 100 | 99 | 100 | 99 | 100 | 100 |
| Social Studies | | | | | | | | | | | | | |
| At least 3 years | 65 | 87 | 86 | 90 | 90 | 90 | 96 | 94 | 98 | 99 | 95 | 93 | 94 |
| At least 4 years | 46 | 78 | 62 | 75 | 50 | 67 | 34 | 62 | 50 | 70 | 45 | 68 | 53 |
| Mathematics | | | | | | | | | | | | | |
| At least 3 years | 19 | 17 | 57 | 24 | 88 | 52 | 96 | 79 | 99 | 95 | 92 | 66 | 82 |
| At least 4 years | 8 | 4 | 27 | 3 | 57 | 14 | 75 | 23 | 84 | 54 | 71 | 24 | 54 |
| Science | | | | | | | | | | | | | |
| At least 3 years | 46 | 4 | 46 | 20 | 71 | 25 | 69 | 32 | 86 | 65 | 74 | 35 | 60 |
| At least 4 years | 8 | 0 | 10 | 7 | 23 | 6 | 24 | 9 | 46 | 58 | 31 | 19 | 27 |
| Foreign Language (Total) | | | | | | | | | | | | | |
| At least 3 years | 4 | 17 | 20 | 37 | 41 | 66 | 44 | 84 | 78 | 97 | 54 | 73 | 61 |
| At least 4 years | 0 | 9 | 11 | 22 | 16 | 46 | 17 | 68 | 19 | 38 | 17 | 46 | 28 |
| One Foreign Language | | | | | | | | | | | | | |
| At least 3 years | 4 | 9 | 14 | 24 | 32 | 44 | 39 | 67 | 73 | 94 | 49 | 59 | 53 |
| At least 4 years | 0 | 0 | 4 | 7 | 6 | 12 | 9 | 29 | 13 | 23 | 10 | 19 | 13 |
| Advanced Placement | | | | | | | | | | | | | |
| English | 0 | 0 | 0 | 0 | 0 | 0 | 1 | 3 | 7 | 7 | 3 | 3 | 3 |
| Languages | 0 | 0 | 0 | 0 | 1 | 0 | 2 | 3 | 5 | 6 | 3 | 2 | 3 |
| Mathematics | 0 | 0 | 0 | 0 | 0 | 0 | 2 | 0 | 11 | 5 | 5 | 1 | 4 |
| Science | 0 | 0 | 0 | 0 | 0 | 0 | 1 | 2 | 8 | 5 | 3 | 2 | 3 |
| Social Studies | 0 | 0 | 0 | 0 | 0 | 0 | 1 | 1 | 5 | 4 | 2 | 1 | 2 |

## Academic Inventories
## (Class of 1959—Grades 9–12)
### 2,182*; Mean I.Q. of Sample: 121

| I.Q. Groupings | 75–89 | | 90–104 | | 105–114 | | 115–129 | | 130 plus | | All I.Q.'s | | |
|---|---|---|---|---|---|---|---|---|---|---|---|---|---|
| Boys—Girls Number | Boy 26 | Girl 23 | Boy 102 | Girl 123 | Boy 213 | Girl 209 | Boy 488 | Girl 255 | Boy 549 | Girl 192 | Boy 1378 | Girl 802 | Total 2180 |
| | | | | | (Figures are per cents) | | | | | | | | |
| **Physics** | | | | | | | | | | | | | |
| At least 1 year | 4 | 0 | 22 | 2 | 47 | 2 | 72 | 11 | 92 | 61 | 71 | 19 | 52 |
| **Combinations** | | | | | | | | | | | | | |
| At least 7 years sci. & math. | 8 | 0 | 22 | 5 | 54 | 7 | 61 | 14 | 83 | 61 | 65 | 22 | 49 |
| At least 7 years Eng. & soc. st. | 65 | 91 | 86 | 91 | 90 | 91 | 95 | 94 | 98 | 99 | 94 | 94 | 94 |
| At least 4 years tot. foreign language, 7 years Eng. & soc. st., 7 years math. and science | 0 | 0 | 6 | 2 | 8 | 2 | 7 | 6 | 12 | 5 | 9 | 4 | 7 |
| **Art** | | | | | | | | | | | | | |
| At least 1 year | 50 | 35 | 39 | 34 | 43 | 38 | 60 | 46 | 86 | 71 | 66 | 48 | 59 |
| At least 2 years | 19 | 26 | 16 | 14 | 15 | 19 | 28 | 21 | 22 | 17 | 23 | 18 | 21 |
| **Music** | | | | | | | | | | | | | |
| At least 1 year | 35 | 30 | 32 | 45 | 42 | 53 | 64 | 47 | 86 | 71 | 67 | 53 | 62 |
| At least 2 years | 23 | 17 | 17 | 24 | 26 | 26 | 48 | 22 | 35 | 7 | 37 | 20 | 30 |
| **Typing** | | | | | | | | | | | | | |
| At least 1 year | 50 | 83 | 35 | 74 | 25 | 59 | 12 | 44 | 3 | 8 | 13 | 45 | 25 |
| At least 2 years | 4 | 26 | 3 | 35 | 0 | 11 | 0 | 4 | 0 | 0 | 0 | 10 | 4 |
| **Business and Secretarial** | | | | | | | | | | | | | |
| At least 1 year | 50 | 83 | 34 | 54 | 23 | 34 | 8 | 19 | 1 | 4 | 10 | 27 | 16 |
| At least 2 years | 35 | 57 | 18 | 44 | 8 | 19 | 3 | 7 | 0 | 1 | 5 | 16 | 9 |
| **Shop (incl. mech. dwg.)** | | | | | | | | | | | | | |
| At least 1 year | 85 | 0 | 59 | 2 | 49 | 3 | 39 | 7 | 57 | 57 | 50 | 17 | 38 |
| At least 2 years | 73 | 0 | 35 | 0 | 23 | 1 | 14 | 0 | 8 | 0 | 16 | 0 | 10 |
| **Home Economics** | | | | | | | | | | | | | |
| At least 1 year | 31 | 87 | 8 | 64 | 5 | 42 | 2 | 24 | 0 | 7 | 3 | 33 | 14 |
| At least 2 years | 15 | 61 | 3 | 28 | 1 | 12 | 0 | 4 | 0 | 1 | 1 | 11 | 4 |
| **Physical Education** | | | | | | | | | | | | | |
| At least 3 years | 92 | 65 | 67 | 76 | 78 | 69 | 84 | 75 | 97 | 96 | 88 | 78 | 84 |
| At least 4 years | 69 | 57 | 59 | 66 | 73 | 64 | 81 | 71 | 96 | 94 | 84 | 73 | 80 |

*Two students in Newton High School below the 75-89 I.Q. level. This category was dropped from the sample.

# TABLE 3:

## The High School Program and Post–High School Occupation of the Typical (Median)* Student in Each I.Q. Group in Six Selected Schools

| I.Q. Group | 75–89 | | | 90–104 | | | 105–114 | | | 115–129 | | | 130+ | | | All I.Q.s | | |
|---|---|---|---|---|---|---|---|---|---|---|---|---|---|---|---|---|---|---|
| Boys—Girls—Total | B | G | T | B | G | T | B | G | T | B | G | T | B | G | T | B | G | T |
| No. in Category | 26 | 23 | 49 | 102 | 123 | 225 | 213 | 209 | 422 | 488 | 255 | 743 | 549 | 192 | 741 | 1378 | 802 | 2180 |
| Post-High School Occupation C—College E—Employed | E | E | E | C | C-E | C | C | C | C | C | C | C | C | C | C | C | C | C |
| *(Figures Are Numbers of Courses Grades 9–12)* | | | | | | | | | | | | | | | | | | |
| **Total Courses** | 22 | 22 | 22 | 22 | 24 | 22 | 23 | 23 | 23 | 24 | 24 | 24 | 26 | 26 | 26 | 24 | 24 | 24 |
| **Total Academic Courses †** | 12 | 12 | 12 | 14 | 14 | 14 | 16 | 16 | 16 | 16 | 18 | 16 | 19 | 19 | 19 | 17 | 17 | 17 |
| 1. English | 4 | 4 | 4 | 4 | 4 | 4 | 4 | 4 | 4 | 4 | 4 | 4 | 4 | 4 | 4 | 4 | 4 | 4 |
| 2. Total Foreign Language | 0 | 0 | 0 | 2 | 2 | 2 | 2 | 3 | 2 | 2 | 4 | 3 | 3 | 3 | 3 | 3 | 3 | 4 |
| 3. Social Studies | 4 | 4 | 4 | 4 | 4 | 4 | 4 | 4 | 4 | 4 | 3 | 4 | 4 | 4 | 4 | 4 | 4 | 4 |
| 4. Mathematics | 2 | 2 | 2 | 3 | 2 | 3 | 3 | 2 | 3 | 3 | 3 | 3 | 4 | 4 | 4 | 4 | 3 | 4 |
| 5. Science | 2 | 2 | 2 | 2 | 2 | 2 | 3 | 2 | 3 | 3 | 2 | 3 | 3 | 4 | 4 | 3 | 2 | 3 |
| **Total Nonacademic Courses †** | 10 | 10 | 10 | 8 | 10 | 8 | 7 | 7 | 7 | 8 | 6 | 8 | 7 | 7 | 7 | 7 | 7 | 7 |
| 1. Physical Education | 4 | 4 | 4 | 4 | 4 | 4 | 4 | 4 | 4 | 4 | 4 | 4 | 4 | 4 | 4 | 4 | 4 | 4 |
| 2. Art, Music, Home Economics, Business and Secretarial, Shop | 6 | 6 | 6 | 4 | 6 | 4 | 3 | 3 | 3 | 4 | 2 | 4 | 3 | 3 | 3 | 3 | 3 | 3 |

* A median represents a midpoint. For example, the typical student takes 24 total courses, but as many students take more than 24 courses as take fewer than 24 total courses. This is another way of looking at the figures presented in the previous table for all six schools combined.

† The totals do not necessarily equal the sum of the individual parts. This happens in a composite picture drawn from different students with different programs. For example, the total academic subjects for all students is 17, but the components add up to 18. With nonacademic subjects, except for physical education, the students distribute themselves so that in few cases do as many as 50 per cent of the students take a particular course.

130

Error of measurement may be involved here, though I suggest that this is dramatic evidence of what I discussed briefly in the last chapter; namely, the variety of colleges and collegiate standards one finds in the United States. My guess is that there is a college somewhere in the United States for any student who graduates from high school. Note the encouragingly high percentage of bright students going to college. Roughly 90 per cent of all the students in the two highest I.Q. categories go on to college—a figure in marked contrast to the situation in at least one state where about 50 per cent of the top quarter fail to develop their talents beyond high school.

Another important observation has to do with the relationship of the number of courses taken to the abilities of the students as determined by tests of scholastic aptitude. There are some people who have criticized my recommendation of a minimum of eighteen academic subjects for academically talented students as too tough a program. These people echo the policy of carrying sixteen academic subjects in four years. There are others who have said that my recommendation is the kind of program that practically all the students should take. I think these inventories furnish some interesting evidence on these points. In the Bronx High School of Science 100 per cent of the boys in the category 115–129 take at least this number of academic courses, and in Newton 84 per cent of the boys in the same category take at least eighteen academic subjects. I submit that this is sufficient evidence to show that such a program is possible without undue hardship on the students involved. It is true that in the other highly motivated academic-minded communities the percentages are lower, but this fact does not mean that my recommendation is impracticable. I venture to suggest that in the high schools throughout the nation the general pattern of four solids a year for bright students might well be broken, that in the interest of the students and the nation these bright young-sters might well take a heavier load.

Leaving aside the Bronx High School of Science, where the program is for the most part required for all students, it is interesting to note in these highly motivated communities the positive relationship between ability and the number of academic subjects taken. The brighter the student, the more academic courses he takes. In Newton three times as many boys in the I.Q. category 130 plus take at least eighteen academic subjects as boys in the category 90–104. I submit that if in an academically oriented town like Newton only 33 per cent of the boys who have *average* ability are taking eighteen academic subjects, it is hopeless to expect most if not all students throughout the nation to take such a program. By definition, half the students in the United States have below-average ability! Until I hear of one public high school in the United States in which for a number of years a majority of average or below-average students have carried at least eighteen academic subjects in four years, and in which high standards are maintained, I shall remain skeptical of currently fashionable claims that the kind of recommendation I have made for the top 15 to 20 per cent should pertain to most if not all students.

A third observation has to do with the well-known fact of the differences between the programs elected by boys and those elected by girls. Note especially total science, mathematics, and physics. To my mind, bright girls, even in these suburban schools, are not taking the program they should in their own and the nation's interests. On the other hand, bright boys are generally neglecting foreign languages.

Whereas there is a positive relationship between ability as measured by scholastic aptitude and academic and total courses taken, there is a negative relationship between scholastic aptitude and nonacademic subjects. One would expect this, of course. The less bright a student, the more likely he is to elect nonacademic courses. Note the distinction that must be made between elective and required courses. English, social studies, and some mathematics and science are generally required in these schools. To be looked at carefully are the sequential nonacademic elective subjects like shop (for the most part industrial arts), secretarial training, and home economics. The reason that only two years were shown for these subjects is that very few students took three- or four-year sequences. I think a question to be raised is the adequacy of the nonacademic elective sequences for students with less-than-average ability.

Table 3 sums up the programs of the typical (median) student, boys and girls separately, in each I.Q. category with all the schools combined. For example, as many boys in the I.Q. range 115–129 were taking more than 24 total courses as were taking fewer than 24. The figure in the table is therefore 24. In other words, this table shows what a typical student in each different ability range is likely to take in the six lighthouse schools, as well as what the typical student, regardless of I.Q. score, is likely to take. Of course, one must remember the skewed distribution of ability in these six schools. The typical student in these schools has an I.Q. of 121 in contrast to the score of about 102 for a typical student in most public high schools—a score which would place him in the bottom quarter of the six schools.

The program for the typical boy in the selected schools is actually very similar to my recommendation for academically talented students, in which category he falls at least on the basis of his test score. He takes a total of twenty-four courses, seventeen of which are academic and seven of which are nonacademic. The academic courses are likely to consist of four years of English, three years of total foreign language (not necessarily one language), three or four years of social studies, four years of mathematics,

and three years of science. With four years of one foreign
language this student's program would meet my recommendation. Aside from four years of physical education, this
typical student takes three courses in art, music, shop, or
other nonacademic subjects. The average girl is likely to
have seventeen academic subjects but two years of science
and three years of mathematics. Both the boy and the girl
are likely to go to college.

Two facts I should like especially to point out have to
do with the number and kind of academic subjects taken.
In these six schools as a whole the magic number of sixteen
Carnegie Units in four years has been broken, at least for
the average students—who, it must be remembered, are
considerably above the national average in terms of ability.
I repeat my plea that the tradition of four academic subjects
a year be examined and, I hope, discarded by accrediting
agencies, state departments of education, and local school
systems. Five academic subjects a year for bright students
are not too much to expect. The second point is that the
tables do show that a broad program that includes foreign
language, science, and mathematics is possible, that many
students are taking such a program without specializing in
one subject at the expense of others. Unless a student does
expand his total program from four to five subjects, some
academic area is bound to suffer.

A final observation has to do with the Bronx High
School of Science. I question somewhat the three years of
a foreign language rather than four, and I would prefer
four years of mathematics to four years of science. Nevertheless, whether one considers total subjects, academic
subjects, or nonacademic subjects, this school stands out.
Granting the exceptional nature of the student body and
the required program, I raise the issue of whether this
extensive program is possible only in a selective academic
high school. I should hope that a climate of opinion could
be created in a comprehensive school that would result

in the same kind of wide program being *elected* by bright students. Students at the Bronx High School of Science take not only a wide program of academic subjects, including English, social studies, mathematics, science, and foreign language—they also take art, music, shop, and physical education. In short, if current proposals for separate schools for talented youth are to be refuted, in my judgment comprehensive high schools across the nation must accept the challenge of providing as sound an education for academically talented youth as that given in the Bronx High School of Science. Earlier I indicated my thought that many suburban schools are accepting this challenge; I hope that all schools will soon do so.

# CHAPTER VI

## Concluding Observations

The dramatic contrasts between schools in the slums and schools in the suburbs illustrate the impossibility of discussing education without specifying the kinds of homes from which the pupils come. Many of the criticisms of the public schools which we have heard in the last few years have ignored this fact. Furthermore, they have been expressed often in terms too general to be constructive. To speak eloquently about raising standards is of little help unless one specifies what kinds of schools one is considering and defines accurately what is meant by the words "academic standards." The critics of American education, so it seems to me, are under an obligation both to be concrete with their proposals and to be clear as to the premises from which they start their arguments. For example, progressive education has become a synonym for all that is bad about our schools. Yet when my own children were young, some thirty and more years ago, progressive education was the new dispensation we were all supposed to acclaim with joy. Referring to an outstanding progressive private elementary school, time and again my friends would say, "If only I could have attended such a school." Today I hear my children's contemporaries condemning their own progressive education and preparing as parents to do their best to see that "It doesn't happen to my children."

Phrases which were once overprized and oversold have come to stand for whatever one doesn't like about our schools. Yet few, if any, of those who bemoan the evil influence of the progressive educators would send their children into the kind of schoolroom which was common sixty years ago. Looking at the pedagogic revolution impartially and historically, one runs into the following stubborn fact. The schools in the forefront of the progressive movement in the first decades of this century were private schools. Close on their heels came the public schools in the high-income suburban areas, where parent-teacher organizations played an effective role in determining what kind of school was kept. Could it be that what the progressive educators thought they had evolved from new philosophic premises was in reality largely a product of a parental revolt against the schools of the nineteenth century? A reforming zeal to provide better schools for one's offspring seems to be the constant factor that unites all the recent generations of American parents. The pendulum swings back and forth with respect to educational slogans.

Professor Cremin of Teachers College, Columbia University, in an excellent book on progressive education, *The Transformation of the School*, has examined American education from 1890 to World War II from the point of view of an historian who understands schools and teachers. He dates the beginning of the progressive movement with the publication of a series of articles in the *Forum* by Joseph M. Rice in 1892, because Rice sought to weave together many separate strands of contemporary protest into a single reform program. Cremin goes on to show how closely the new educational developments of the next three decades were tied to the reform movement in politics and the social concern of such people as Jane Addams. Progressive education on examination he declares "turns out to be nothing less than the educational phase of America's progressivism writ large." Of this phase John Dewey became a major prophet, but he was in no sense the founder, nor were those who were experimenting with new classroom techniques in 1910 all his disciples.

Indeed I think it is illuminating to turn back the pages of history to the 1870s to see what was being done in Quincy, Massachusetts, by a man whom John Dewey once called the father of progressive education. The school board of that New England town, largely under the influence of Charles Francis Adams, the son of the statesman and diplomat of the Civil War period, had engaged one Col. Francis W. Parker as superintendent. This former officer in the Union Army had studied pedagogy in Germany and developed some radical ideas of his own. He and the school board appeared to see eye to eye, and what they accomplished between 1875 and 1879 is told by Mr. Adams in an address which, to me, is of fascinating interest since it presents so vividly the contrast between the old and the new pedagogic approach to the education of young children.

A series of examinations introduced in 1873 had convinced the members of the Quincy school committee that the pupils could "neither speak nor spell their own language very perfectly, nor read and write it with the ease and elegance which is desirable." According to Mr. Adams, the examinations had shown in fact that in far too many cases those examined "could neither read nor write at all!" Then a new system was introduced by Colonel Parker. "The essence of the new system was that there was no system about it; it was marked throughout by intense individuality. . . . Experiments were to be cautiously tried and results from time to time noted." As a school board member Mr. Adams emphasized the cautious approach, also the economical one, but what he actually reports must have sounded radical enough. "The old 'dame school' disappeared at once. In place of it appeared something as different as light from darkness. The alphabet itself was no longer taught . . . little ones were learning to read almost without knowing it . . . a play-table and toys were furnished them . . . the children actually went to school without being dragged there. Yet the reason for this was not far to seek. The simple fact was that they were happier and more amused and better contented at school than at home. The drudgery of the impossible primer no longer made infant life miserable. The alphabet was robbed of its terrors, and stole upon them unawares."

The Quincy reforms were not confined to the first grade, however. The teaching of geography was enlivened by having the children make three-dimensional maps with moistened clay. As an upshot of all the changes, Mr. Adams reports that "the children had ceased to dislike their schoolrooms; and to those who remember as vividly as most persons over thirty do, the whole unattractive, not to say repulsive character both of the old-time school teaching and the old-time school discipline, this change is one for which those who enjoy the advantage of it may well be grateful."

Colonel Parker left Quincy for Boston the year following Mr. Adams' glowing report, and in 1893 moved to Chicago, where he and Dewey came to know each other—which had far-reaching effects on American education. If one reads Colonel Parker's *Talks on Pedagogics* published in 1894 and John Dewey's *School and Society* published in 1899, the influence of the older school man with a rich teaching experience on the young philosopher is clearly evident. Dewey, and later his followers who were professors of education, added several elements of importance to the new pedagogic approaches of the 1890s and early 1900s. Indeed by 1919, when the Progressive Education Association was founded, the movement had acquired much ideological baggage, some of it related to psychology, some to sociology, and not a little to politics as well. The latter was to prove to be an awkward load to carry and by no means as closely related to the basic principle as was at first maintained. Indeed, since the new pedagogic approach was early accepted in the elementary schools, it would be my contention that the permanent influence of the movement is to be found by examining what actually goes on in the classroom and not what professors of education have had to say about it. In other words, it is important to separate the new techniques of teaching from some of the wider aims of the progressive movement, particularly from those which were manifest in the depression years. To this end, I should like to distinguish sharply between elementary schools and secondary schools.

Confining attention, for the moment then, to the education of young children, I believe any impartial investigator would say that the contrast painted so long ago by Mr. Adams in Quincy would be the contrast between a vast majority of schools in the 1890s and the schools in the 1960s. The major reforms of elementary education which have taken place seem so obvious today that I would challenge anyone to try and set up a school which negated them. Call it a child-centered school, or a humane school, or use Adams' phrase and characterize it as a school "the children had ceased to dislike," the advantages of the new type of school and the new attitude of teachers as compared with the typical school of the late nineteenth century are just not open to argument by anyone familiar with the facts. I am not speaking of particular teaching methods, for example the teaching of reading, but of general methods used by teachers to enlist the interest and enthusiasm of children.

There are many things about our schools today which I join with others in severely criticizing. Some of them can be attributed to those educators who were in the forefront of the progressive movement. Many others are the consequences of parental desires of the 1920s and 1930s which were a reaction against the "too-bookish" schooling of their youth. Some of the critics are fond of comparing the American public high school with either the British Grammar Schools or German Gymnasia today or the American high schools of 1900. To make this comparison is to ignore a second revolution in American education which I have called the transformation of the high school. This transformation was a consequence of the radical change in the laws and customs affecting the employment of youth. A realization of this social change is so basic to an understanding of the problems of secondary education that I shall attempt to summarize a large bit of American history in a few short paragraphs.

Those of us who remember the period between the Spanish-American War and World War I will readily recall both the optimism of those days and the radical discontent. The two went together. Writers and some political figures were highly critical of the American society which they saw around them. The new waves of immigrants which kept arriving in the last decades of the nineteenth century brought people much more difficult to assimilate than those who had arrived in the 1840s and 1850s. In cities and towns where the new settlers clustered, language barriers were overcome with difficulty. In one mining town in northern Minnesota in 1905, I have been told, there were more than a dozen nationalities speaking a dozen different languages.

In the big cities the foreigners were housed in crowded, impoverished, and frightfully unsanitary slums. Cleaning up the slums, Americanizing the immigrants (adults and children) through formal schools and settlement houses, and reforming the corrupt politics of the cities were tasks which seemed urgent to all right-thinking people of the day. The progressive in politics and the conservative agreed on the need for changing many shocking social situations. On certain topics such as trust-busting, the initiative and referendum, women's suffrage, governmental regulation of railroads, and the recall of judicial decisions, there was anything but agreement among the leaders of opinion. Those who considered themselves progressive in politics and who followed Theodore Roosevelt's banner in 1912 would have

been in favor of most if not all the reforms I have just
listed and would have added conservation of national resources spelled with large and flaming letters. Part and
parcel of the progressive movement in politics were efforts
to do something about child labor.

When the industrialization of the Eastern states first
started, early in the nineteenth century, the laboring force
for the mills was recruited from the nearby farms. On farms
children as well as youth had always been expected to work
long hours. Therefore, to the first few generations of industrialized Americans, it was not strange that in the new
mills children as well as adults found employment and
worked from dawn to dusk. The same situation had developed still earlier in Great Britain and gradually aroused the
social conscience of that nation. The demand for the regulation of the factory work of women and children had
been voiced on the other side of the Atlantic long before
the nineteenth century was over, as readers of Dickens
and his contempories well know.

Here in the United States the movement to abolish
child labor did not gain momentum until the era of progressivism began. Then regulation of working conditions
and the elimination of children from the mills became one
of the more important objectives of the reformers. Progress
was slow, however, and when in 1916 Congress passed a
law prohibiting child labor, the Supreme Court declared
the law unconstitutional. But state laws were passed and,
more important, the climate of opinion was in process of
rapid change. Management and labor altered their attitudes
towards the employment of young people. Long before
the passage of the New Deal legislation which abolished
child labor in factories, public opinion in most parts of the
country had demanded that all children be educated before
they were sent to work.

Writing in 1902, a professor of education at the University of California said, "Primary education . . . is the

education needed for all; which, for the sake of the general good, no citizen can be permitted to do without. Beyond this is the region of difference, of divergence, and it may be added, of very great uncertainty and dispute. Occasionally one hears the prophecy that what we call secondary education will eventually be an education for all." Here was a professional educator at the beginning of the twentieth century wondering if secondary education might some day be education for all, which it certainly was not at that time. Forty years later the Educational Policies Commission of the National Education Association published a book entitled *Education for All American Youth*. While many disagreed with the prescriptions contained in this volume, few if any challenged the title. Four decades had completed the transformation of American secondary schools. Despite the "uncertainty and dispute" that continued to persist, secondary schools became institutions providing full-time schooling for all youth.

Taking the country as a whole, we find in 1910 that some 30 per cent of the youth fourteen and fifteen years of age were employed; twenty years later the figure had dropped to 9 per cent. In the same period, the percentage of youth sixteen and seventeen years old who were employed was cut in half (from 66 to 32 per cent). As the employed figure diminished, the school enrollments increased. The alterations proceeded at a different rate in different communities, but by World War I it was clear that before long the nature of the secondary school population was going to be very different from what it had been when the century began. It is hardly necessary to argue that the change was irreversible. Anyone who doubts this can try to persuade Congress and the state legislatures to repeal the mass of laws that now restrict the opportunities for young people to get jobs. Whether the teacher liked it or not, the high schools were forced to become schools for all. Today 80 per cent of the youth ages sixteen and seventeen are in school. What this fact has meant for the curriculum and organization of the schools raises not one question but many questions. After forty years we are still arguing about the answers.

How we attempt today to provide education is a consequence of the new ideas of those who led progressive education and the subsequent reaction to these ideas. Why we attempt to provide education for *all* American youth is fundamentally a consequence of a basic change in the social and economic pattern of our society. The extreme examples of high schools I have discussed in the preceding chapters and the perplexing problems facing the teachers in these schools illustrate the wide range of complexities American educators must face. Few in the profession would claim they knew the answers to these complexities. Few would maintain that even with ample resources they were providing a satisfactory education for every one of their students. Therefore they always welcome informed criticism, reserving the right to challenge the critic as to his premises and, particularly, as to the validity of any arguments based on comparisons between schools in different communities, even different communities within a single state. My own premises, I trust, I have made evident. If so, I may then claim the privilege of summing up my conclusions about schools in suburbs and in slums.

## Summary

As to the schools in the well-to-do suburbs:

1. The main problem in wealthy suburban schools is to guide the parent whose college ambitions outrun his child's abilities toward a realistic picture of the kind of college his child is suited for.

2. Expert guidance must begin very early in the suburban schools in this process of educating both parent and child in the realities of college admission.

3. The prestige colleges should be seen as institutions for very bright students, the majority of whom will go to graduate school for advanced degrees. Many will enter the professions.

4. The California pattern of higher education, which includes two-year junior colleges, should be examined with care by citizens interested in solving college problems within many states.

5. The place to begin to set standards in American education is at the last rung of the educational ladder— the graduate level. Requirements for admission to law and medical schools and to graduate schools of arts and sciences should include evidence by examination of a wide and solid academic education. The requirements might be as follows: the ability to write a competent essay; a good reading, writing, and speaking knowledge of at least one modern foreign language; a knowledge of mathematics through the calculus; a knowledge of physics, chemistry, and biology at the freshman level of our most rigorous colleges; at the same level of competence, knowledge of American history and political institutions and English and American literature. The implementation of this recommendation might well have a salutary effect upon the education of bright students in both schools and colleges by bringing about what is called for in recommendation 6.

6. All high schools should try to create a climate of opinion that will encourage bright students to elect the kind of wide program that is required of students in the Bronx High School of Science. Such a program means five rather than the traditional four academic subjects a year.

7. Every high school ought to strive for participation in the Advanced Placement Program.

As to the schools in the large city slums:

8. The contrast in the money spent per pupil in wealthy suburban schools and in slum schools of the large

cities challenges the concept of equality of opportunity in American public education. More money is needed in slum schools.

9. Social dynamite is building up in our large cities in the form of unemployed out-of-school youth, especially in the Negro slums. We need accurate and frank information neighborhood by neighborhood.

10. The schools should be given the responsibility for educational and vocational guidance of youth after they leave school until age 21. This will require more money.

11. Increased attention ought to be paid in both slums and suburbs to developing meaningful courses for pupils with less than average abilities. To this end consideration should be given by every school and community to the expansion of work-study programs for slow students, and to the provision of at least an auto mechanics shop for boys in every high school in metropolitan areas.

12. Employment opportunities in the large cities must be promptly opened on a non-discriminatory basis. Because of the attitude of management and labor this can be done only through the use of federal funds.

13. The answer to improving Negro education in the large Northern cities is to spend more money and to upgrade Negro schools, many of which are in slums, rather than to effect token integration by transporting pupils across attendance lines. Fully integrated teaching staffs are a necessity as well.

14. More teachers and perhaps more pay for teachers are necessary for schools in the slums than in either the high income districts of the large cities or the wealthy suburbs. Special training programs for teachers in slum schools are needed.

15. No effort should be spared in slum areas to enlist the support of parents in the education of their children. To

this end, adult education programs should be improved and expanded.

16. Big cities need decentralized administration in order to bring the schools closer to the needs of the people in each neighborhood and to make each school fit the local situation.

17. Nonpolitical, honest school boards composed of high-minded citizens who can differentiate between policy-making and administration are essential. An aroused public opinion is needed to correct the situation in those cities where such school boards do not exist.

I have sought to create a set of anxious thoughts in the minds of the conscientious citizens who may read these pages and who, while living in the suburbs, may work in the city. To improve the work of the slum schools requires an improvement in the lives of the families who inhabit the slums, but without a drastic change in the employment prospects for urban Negro youth, relatively little can be accomplished. Therefore I close by urging that our large city educational problems be analyzed in far more detail than in the past and with a far greater degree of frank-ness. Neighborhood by neighborhood we need to know the facts, and when these facts indicate a dangerous social situation the American people should be prepared to take prompt action before it is too late.